OMNIPRESENT

THE ENTREPRENEUR EVERYONE KNOWS...

MASTER. JAMAR Z BERRY

LONDON BY DESIGN PUBLISHING HOUSE LTD.

2022

COPYRIGHT

Publication © 2025 by London By Design Publishing House Ltd.
Contact Details:
LondonByDesignPublishing@gmail.com

ISBN: 978-1-998583-03-4

Book Description

Unlock the secrets to entrepreneurial greatness with "OMNIPRESENT: THE ENTREPRENEUR EVERYONE KNOWS..." by Jamar Berry. This inspirational guide is crafted for those who aspire to take their business game to new heights, empowering you with the mindset and strategies to think and act like a millionaire or billionaire.

In this transformative book, you'll explore the Omnipresent Entrepreneurial Mindset that sets successful leaders apart. Discover how to harness the power of perspective, ambition, and discipline to not just navigate, but thrive amid challenges. Each chapter is packed with innovative insights on turning adversity into opportunity while teaching you to embrace change and see potential where others fail to look.

Delve into the unconventional strategies that can elevate your business, from networking like a pro to creating a high-performance mindset. Learn how to build a reputation that stands out and makes you unforgettable in your industry. As you climb the ladder of success, you'll find inspiration in the stories of trailblazers who have left an indelible mark on the entrepreneurial landscape.

Jamar Berry emphasizes the importance of resilience, wellness, and ethical practices in the pursuit of success. You'll gain tools for personal growth, including ways to overcome imposter syndrome and foster empowerment in your team. The focus on sustainable success ensures that your journey will not only elevate your business but also create a lasting impact on your community.

Whether you're a budding entrepreneur or an established business leader, "OMNIPRESENT" is your roadmap to creating a powerful legacy. Get ready to embrace the joy of the journey, redefine what success means to you, and become the entrepreneur everyone knows—not just for your achievements but for the positive influence you wield. Your journey to omnipresence starts now!

Table of Contents

Chapter 1

The Power of Perspective

Understanding different viewpoints and using
empathy to connect.

In the ever-evolving landscape of entrepreneurship, the ability to understand and appreciate different viewpoints becomes an indispensable asset. The journey of an entrepreneur is often marked by challenges, uncertainties, and the need for decisive action. Yet, amid these pressures, the most successful leaders have mastered an essential skill: the art of perspective. By developing a broader understanding of various viewpoints, entrepreneurs can foster empathy, strengthen relationships, and drive their businesses forward in profound ways.

The Lens of Perspective

Perspective is defined as a particular attitude toward or way of regarding something; it is a point of view. Each individual perceives the world through a unique lens that has been shaped by their experiences, culture, education, and values. As entrepreneurs, recognizing that your perspective is not the only narrative is crucial. Different perspectives offer fresh insights, challenge assumptions, and lead to innovative solutions.

Imagine a complex puzzle, where each piece represents a different viewpoint. You may have a unique way to see the situation; however, when other perspectives are added, the full picture begins to emerge. Limiting oneself to a singular viewpoint can hinder growth and creativity, whereas embracing diverse perspectives opens the door to a treasure trove of ideas and inspiration.

Empathy: The Bridge to Connection

Empathy, the ability to understand and share the feelings of another, is a critical component of effective perspective-taking. For entrepreneurs, empathy is not just a soft skill; it is a powerful tool that influences decision-making and strengthens connections with customers, employees, and stakeholders.

When you actively listen to others and attempt to understand their feelings and experiences, you build trust and rapport. Whether it's a dissatisfied customer, a business partner with a different vision, or a team member facing challenges, approaching these interactions with empathy allows you to engage meaningfully. Empathetic entrepreneurs create an environment where individuals feel valued, leading to heightened loyalty, collaboration, and creativity.

The Importance of Diverse Teams

One of the most effective ways to cultivate diverse perspectives is to assemble a team that reflects a variety of backgrounds, experiences, and skillsets. Businesses led by diverse teams benefit from enhanced problem-solving abilities and improved innovation. According to a study by McKinsey & Company, companies in the top quartile for gender and ethnic diversity are 15% and 35% more likely to have above-average profitability, respectively.

By encouraging open dialogue and creating a culture where all voices are welcomed, entrepreneurs can tap into the unique strengths of a diverse team. This not only leads to better decision-making but also fosters an inclusive atmosphere where creativity flourishes. Each team member contributes their perspective, and together, they can navigate challenges with greater insight and adaptability.

Real-World Applications of Perspective

Understanding the practical implications of perspective can be transformative for entrepreneurs. Here are several real-world applications where perspective can significantly impact outcomes:

1. **Customer Experience**: Customers come from different backgrounds and have unique needs and expectations. By empathizing with their experiences, entrepreneurs can design products and services that resonate more profoundly with their target audience. For instance, a tech company that engages with users from diverse communities can uncover essential feedback that informs product development. Harnessing different customer perspectives not only enhances user experience but grows loyalty and fosters brand advocacy.

2. **Conflict Resolution**: Conflicts are an unavoidable aspect of any business. When tensions arise, the initial instinct may be to defend one's position. However, great leaders recognize that adopting an empathetic viewpoint can lead to resolution rather than escalation. When addressing conflicts with an open mind and a willingness to understand the other side, entrepreneurs can find common ground and solution-focused pathways.

3. **Strategic Decision-Making**: Strategic decisions can significantly impact the future of a business. When entrepreneurs evaluate different angles and perspectives on critical issues, they can make more informed and balanced decisions. Considering various stakeholder viewpoints—such as customers, employees, investors, and the community—provides greater clarity on potential risks and benefits.

4. **Marketing and Branding**: The essence of successful marketing lies in understanding the audience. Empathizing with consumers' emotions and cultural contexts can enhance campaigns. For instance, a socially-conscious brand that incorporates diverse perspectives into its messaging and branding will likely resonate more deeply with its audience, establishing a connection built on shared values.

Cultivating Perspective: Techniques and Exercises

To harness the power of perspective effectively, entrepreneurs can implement several techniques:

1. **Active Listening**: Engage in active listening during conversations. Allow the other person to express themselves fully without interruption. Respond by paraphrasing or summarizing what they've said to demonstrate understanding.

2. **Seek Feedback**: Encourage honest feedback from team members, customers, and mentors. A culture that embraces constructive criticism allows various perspectives to be shared openly.

3. **Diverse Networks**: Attend networking events and seek out diverse groups. Engaging with individuals

from different industries and cultures broadens your horizon and allows for growth in your thinking.

4. **Journaling**: Maintain a reflective journal where you explore different viewpoints on challenges

5. **Role Reversal**: Engage in role-playing exercises with team members or peers to gain insights into their perspectives. By advocating for another person's viewpoint, you can deepen your understanding of their needs, concerns, and motivations.

6. **Mentorship**: Seek a mentor who has a different background or perspective than you. Their unique insights can offer guidance tailored to various situations and help you navigate complex challenges.

7. **Diversity Training**: Consider investing in diversity training programs that educate team members about cultural competence and the importance of various perspectives. This can create a more inclusive workplace culture.

8. **Cultivating Curiosity**: Foster a mindset of curiosity by asking open-ended questions. Encourage your team to explore answers together, as this can lead to discovering new facets of problems and solutions.

The Ripple Effect of Perspective

The impact of cultivating perspective extends beyond individual interactions. It creates a ripple effect that permeates the entire organization. As leaders model empathy and perspective-taking, they inspire a culture in which every team member feels empowered to express their ideas and challenges. This collaborative atmosphere reduces turnover, increases morale, and cultivates loyalty among employees.

Additionally, organizations that prioritize empathy and perspective foster a positive impact beyond their walls. A company that takes the time to understand and address community needs not only enhances its reputation but also contributes to a more engaged and supportive customer base. When businesses exemplify a commitment to understanding various viewpoints, they build lasting relationships that go beyond mere transactions.

The Entrepreneurial Journey: A Perspective Shift

Entrepreneurship is inherently defined by constant change and adaptation. As you navigate your journey, it's essential to maintain a mindset open to growth, learning, and perspective shifts. Developing this flexibility will enable you to embrace the unexpected and pivot when necessary.

Consider the journey of a successful entrepreneur who faced numerous roadblocks. Instead of viewing these challenges as failures, they adopted a perspective of learning opportunities. By analyzing setbacks through different lenses and actively seeking feedback, they could recalibrate their strategy and outmaneuver obstacles more effectively. This mindset not only led to personal growth but also cultivated a resilient team ready to innovate and thrive in adversity.

As we close this chapter, reflect on the immense potential that comes from harnessing the power of perspective. As an entrepreneur, your ability to understand and appreciate diverse viewpoints will serve as a cornerstone for your growth, success, and overall impact. By fostering empathy within your organization and extending it to your community, you can create a legacy that influences and uplifts those around you.

Ultimately, it is through the lens of perspective that we can truly connect, innovate, and lead. The journey ahead will be filled with numerous opportunities to apply these lessons, and by embracing various viewpoints, you will position yourself not only as an entrepreneur of note but as a catalyst for change, understanding, and progress.

By mastering the power of perspective, you become equipped to navigate the complexities of entrepreneurship and inspired to make decisions that resonate deeply with others. As you embark on the path of being the entrepreneur everyone knows, let this chapter serve as a reminder that the richness of your journey lies not just in your achievements but in your ability to connect, empathize, and understand the diverse human experience around you.

Chapter 2

The Energy of Ambition

Harnessing ambition to fuel your entrepreneurial journey.

Ambition is often described as the driving force behind success, serving as both the fuel and the compass for the entrepreneurial journey. It is an innate desire to achieve greatness, surpass limitations, and reach new heights. While ambition can take on many forms, its essence remains the same: a relentless pursuit of excellence. In this chapter, we will explore the concept of ambition, how it can energize your entrepreneurial endeavors, and how to channel it effectively to propel your business forward.

Understanding Ambition

At its core, ambition is the strong desire to accomplish something. It is what pushes individuals to strive for goals, overcome challenges, and improve their circumstances. In the world of entrepreneurship, ambition manifests in various ways, such as setting audacious business goals, pursuing innovative solutions, and yearning for continuous growth. However, ambition must be carefully balanced; unchecked, it can lead to burnout, unethical decisions, and neglect of essential relationships.

Ambition is often associated with positive traits like determination, motivation, and resilience. It fuels creativity and innovation, urging entrepreneurs to identify opportunities where others see obstacles. This energy not only inspires individuals but also has the potential to galvanize entire teams, creating a collective momentum that drives progress.

Harnessing the Energy of Ambition

1. **Setting Clear Goals**

The first step in harnessing the energy of ambition is to define clear, measurable, and specific goals. Ambition thrives within a structured framework, and without goals, it can become aimless. Consider adopting the SMART criteria for goal-setting—ensuring that your objectives are Specific, Measurable, Achievable, Relevant, and Time-bound. This clarity allows you to channel your ambition effectively, directing your efforts toward tangible outcomes.

For instance, rather than simply striving to increase revenue, an ambitious goal might be to achieve a 25% increase in sales over the next fiscal year by launching a new product or expanding into a new market. This clear goal creates a roadmap for your ambitious pursuits and provides direction.

2. **Embracing a Growth Mindset**

A growth mindset, which emphasizes the belief that skills and intelligence can be developed through hard work and dedication, is essential for ambitious entrepreneurs. Embracing this mindset allows you to view challenges as opportunities for learning and improvement. Rather than feeling threatened by unforeseen obstacles, you can approach them with curiosity and a willingness to adapt.

When faced with setbacks, reflect on what can be learned. For instance, if a marketing campaign fails to generate expected results, analyze the data to understand why and adjust your strategy accordingly. This approach not only enhances resilience but also fuels your ambitious energy by transforming failures into stepping stones toward success.

3. Surrounding Yourself with Inspiration

The company you keep plays a critical role in shaping your ambitions. Surrounding yourself with individuals who inspire and uplift you can exponentially increase your energy levels. Seek out mentors, peers, and thought leaders who embody the qualities and achievements you aspire to emulate.

Participating in mastermind groups or networking events can expose you to different perspectives and experiences that broaden your horizons. The energy within these interactions can ignite your own ambition, sparking new ideas and potential collaborations that can elevate your business further.

4. Taking Action

Ambition without action is like fuel without fire. It is crucial to translate your ambitious desires into concrete steps. Break your long-term goals into smaller, actionable tasks. Maintain momentum by celebrating small wins along the way—they reinforce your commitment and energize your journey.

Set regular checkpoints to assess your progress, adjusting your path as necessary. This proactive approach allows you to maintain your ambitious drive, as each accomplishment builds confidence and provides renewed motivation.

The Dual Nature of Ambition

While ambition is an essential ingredient for success, it is essential to recognize that it has a dual nature. On one hand, it can lead to extraordinary achievements; on the other, it can result in destructive behaviors if left unchecked. It is crucial to strike a balance—pursuing goals with zeal while remaining mindful of the impact on yourself and those around you.

1. **Balancing Personal and Professional Life**

The relentless pursuit of ambition can create a tendency to prioritize work over personal well-being. While striving for excellence is admirable, neglecting life outside of work can lead to burnout and dissatisfaction. Maintain a holistic approach by integrating self-care practices, fostering relationships with loved ones, and pursuing interests outside of entrepreneurship.

Schedule downtime, engage in hobbies, and spend time with family and friends. This balance improves overall well-being and resilience, allowing your ambitious energy to flourish rather than wane.

2. **Ethical Considerations**

Ambition can become detrimental when it leads to unethical decisions or cutthroat behavior. As entrepreneurs, success should not come at the expense of integrity or the well-being of others. Uphold your core values and establish ethical guidelines for your business practices. Remember that true ambition seeks lasting success characterized by respect, trust, and positive contributions to the community.

Fueling Your Ambition

1. **Passion as a Catalyst**

Passion acts as a driving force behind ambition, providing the energy needed to overcome obstacles and stay committed to your goals. When you are passionate about what you do, your enthusiasm becomes infectious, inspiring those around you. This intrinsic motivation fuels creativity and fosters perseverance, making it easier to navigate the inevitable challenges of entrepreneurship.

Identify your passions and align them with your business goals. Ask yourself: What excites you? What problems do you genuinely want to solve? When your ambitions are tied to your passions, the pursuit becomes more fulfilling and energizing. For example, a chef who is passionate about farm-to-table practices is not only driven by the goal of running a successful restaurant but is also motivated by a love for sustainability and quality food.

2. **Visualizing Success**

Visualization is a powerful technique that ambitious entrepreneurs can use to keep their focus sharp and their energy levels high. By envisioning your desired outcomes, you can create a mental blueprint that guides your actions. Spend time each day imagining yourself achieving your goals—whether launching a successful product, securing a significant investment, or leading a high-performing team.

This practice not only strengthens your resolve but also helps you identify the steps needed to turn your vision into reality. Visualization primes your mind for success, boosting your confidence and reminding you of the possibilities that await you.

3. **Embracing Lifelong Learning**

The entrepreneurial landscape is dynamic and constantly changing. To stay ahead, ambitious entrepreneurs must commit to lifelong learning and skill development. Pursue online courses, attend workshops, read industry-related books, and engage in continuous professional development. This commitment not only enhances your knowledge but keeps your ambition fresh and excited.

Moreover, seeking knowledge from various fields—such as psychology, technology, and economics—can provide valuable insights that sharpen your competitive edge. The more you learn, the more equipped you become to navigate challenges and seize new opportunities.

The Collective Ambition of Your Team

As an entrepreneur, your ambition may be the spark that ignites your journey, but it is crucial to ignite the collective ambition of your team as well. When every member of your organization shares a common vision and purpose, the energy multiplies, leading to significant momentum.

1. Creating a Visionary Culture

A clearly articulated vision serves as a rallying point, uniting your team around shared goals and aspirations. Create an environment where employees feel invested in the company's success. Encourage open communication and solicit input from your team. When individuals know their contributions matter, their ambition grows, further energizing the entire organization.

Host regular team meetings to discuss progress toward goals, celebrate achievements, and brainstorm new initiatives. This culture of collaboration fosters enthusiasm and keeps everyone focused on the collective vision.

2. Recognizing and Rewarding Ambition

Positive reinforcement plays an essential role in nurturing ambition within your team. Celebrate accomplishments, no matter how small, and recognize individuals who embody the spirit of ambition. Whether through public acknowledgment, performance bonuses, or opportunities for professional growth, showing appreciation can motivate others to pursue their goals with vigor.

Creating pathways for advancement allows team members to see the potential for growth within your organization. This not only helps retain talent but also fosters a culture of ambition that drives innovation and productivity.

As we conclude this chapter on the energy of ambition, it is clear that ambition is a powerful force that can propel entrepreneurs toward greatness. By setting clear goals, embracing a growth mindset, surrounding yourself with motivation, and taking decisive action, you harness this energy to achieve extraordinary outcomes. However, it is crucial to navigate ambition with care, balancing your personal well-being, upholding ethical standards, and fostering a supportive culture within your organization.

Remember that ambition is not merely a personal trait; it is a collective journey—one that can foster innovation, inspire those around you, and create a positive impact on your community. Your ambition has the power to change not only your life but also the lives of others.

As you embark on your entrepreneurial path, let your ambition be the driving force that ignites your passion and propels you forward. Embrace the challenges, seize the opportunities, and channel your ambition into creating a legacy that will inspire generations to come. With this mindset, you become not just an entrepreneur but a leader of impact—an architect of change in a world that thrives on vision and ambition.

Reflection

Take a moment to reflect on your ambitions. What excites you most about your entrepreneurial journey? How can you sustain that energy in the long term? Write down your thoughts, refine your goals, and commit to the path ahead. The journey of a thousand miles begins with a single step, and with every step fueled by ambition, you move closer to becoming the entrepreneur everyone knows and admires.

Chapter 3

From Inspiration to Action

Transforming ideas into tangible results with structured action.

In the realm of entrepreneurship, inspiration can often feel like a double-edged sword. It fuels creativity, ignites passion, and prompts innovation, yet it can also lead to inertia if not transformed into meaningful action. The ability to turn inspired thoughts into concrete steps is what truly sets successful entrepreneurs apart. In this chapter, we will dive into the journey from inspiration to action, exploring techniques, mindset shifts, and the importance of accountability that can help entrepreneurs capitalize on their ideas and create lasting impact.

The Nature of Inspiration

Inspiration can strike at any moment, whether during a quiet moment of reflection, a casual conversation with a friend, or while reading an insightful book. It serves as a spark—an immediate rush of excitement that opens the door to new possibilities. However, inspiration alone is not enough. It requires cultivation and direction to yield fruitful results.

Think of inspiration as the initial brushstroke on a blank canvas. While it sets the tone, the beauty of the masterpiece emerges only through a series of intentional actions. The challenge lies in capturing that initial burst of enthusiasm and directing it into a structured plan for implementation.

Identifying Your Sources of Inspiration

Before you can harness inspiration, it's vital to identify what ignites your creative energy. Reflect on the experiences, environments, and people that inspire you. Consider keeping a journal where you document moments of inspiration— ideas that excite you, insights that resonate deeply, and problems you wish to solve.

1. **Creative Environments**: Surround yourself with spaces that encourage creativity. This could be a coffee shop, a park, or even a dedicated workspace filled with inspiring visuals and motivational quotes. Your environment plays a significant role in cultivating inspiration.

2. **Role Models**: Engage with successful entrepreneurs and creators through books, podcasts, or interviews. Learn about their journeys, challenges, and triumphs. Their stories can spark new ideas and motivate you to take action.

3. **Engage in Diverse Experiences**: Explore new activities, hobbies, or interests outside your field. These varied experiences can stimulate your thinking and lead to unexpected insights applicable to your business.

Translating Inspiration into Action

Once you've captured inspiration, the next step is to transform those ideas into actionable steps. Here's a strategic approach to bridging the gap between inspiration and action:

1. **Brainstorming and Mind Mapping**

Begin by brainstorming your ideas. Gather all your inspired concepts on paper or a digital platform. Use mind mapping techniques to organize your thoughts visually. This process not only clarifies your ideas but helps you identify potential pathways for implementation.

For example, if you were inspired to create a new product, map out associated concepts like target audience, features, delivery methods, and potential challenges. Visualizing connections can spark additional ideas and create a comprehensive roadmap for action.

2. **Break It Down**

Taking inspired action can feel overwhelming, especially if the vision seems expansive. Break your primary goal down into smaller, manageable tasks. Create a timeline that outlines the steps required to bring your vision to life.

Using the product example again, tasks might include market research, prototyping, and developing a marketing strategy. By segmenting the process, you can tackle one task at a time, making it easier to stay motivated.

3. **Set Milestones and Deadlines**

To maintain momentum, establish milestones—specific targets designed to track your progress. Assign deadlines to these milestones to encourage accountability. This creates a sense of urgency and keeps your enthusiasm alive as you check off completed objectives.

For instance, if your goal is to launch a new service in six months, you might set milestones such as completing a business plan within the first month, finalizing branding by the second month, and launching a beta version by the fourth month.

The Role of Mindset in Action

1. ### Overcoming Fear of Failure

The fear of failure often acts as a barrier to action, leading many aspiring entrepreneurs to hold back on pursuing their ideas. It's essential to reframe failure as a natural part of the learning process. Instead of fearing mistakes, embrace the notion that every setback provides valuable lessons that can inform and enhance future efforts.

Cultivating a "fail-forward" mentality—where each failure acts as a stepping stone to success—will empower you to take informed risks. Renowned entrepreneurs like Thomas Edison understood this concept well, famously stating, "I have not failed. I've just found 10,000 ways that won't work." Adopting a similar perspective allows you to shift your focus from perfection to progress.

2. ### Cultivating Resilience

A successful entrepreneurial journey requires resilience— the ability to bounce back from setbacks and adapt to change. As you take action, challenges will inevitably arise. Building resilience involves maintaining a positive outlook and developing coping strategies to navigate difficulties.

Consider establishing a support network of fellow entrepreneurs or mentors who understand the challenges you face. They can offer guidance, motivation, and camaraderie during tough times, reminding you that you are not alone in the journey.

Accountability: The Catalyst for Action

While inspiration and planning are crucial, accountability is the driving force that propels entrepreneurs from contemplation to action. Having someone—or a mechanism—in place to hold you accountable creates a sense of responsibility that enhances your commitment to transforming your ideas into reality.

1. Finding an Accountability Partner

Consider finding an accountability partner who shares similar goals or aspirations. Regular check-ins—whether weekly or biweekly—can help keep you on track. In these meetings, discuss your progress, share challenges, and celebrate achievements. This mutual support encourages perseverance and helps you maintain momentum.

2. Utilizing Technology and Tools

Leverage modern technology to enhance accountability. Utilize apps and tools designed for project management, such as Trello, Asana, or Monday.com. These platforms allow you to set deadlines, assign tasks, and track progress transparently. By documenting your journey in real time, you create a roadmap you can reference and adjust as needed.

3. Public Commitment

Making a public commitment to your goals can increase your accountability significantly. Share your ambitions with friends, family, or social media networks. When others are aware of your goals, the desire to follow through often intensifies. Additionally, you may find support and encouragement from those who want to see you succeed.

4. Reflect on Progress

Integrate regular reflection into your schedule to assess your progress. Dedicate time each week or month to evaluate what's working and what needs adjustment. Ask yourself the following questions:

- What milestones have I accomplished?

- Where did I encounter obstacles?

- What lessons have I learned from challenges?

This reflection will reinforce your commitment, realign your focus, and ensure that you remain on track with your plans. It's essential to be honest with yourself during this process and to adapt your strategies as necessary.

Staying Inspired

Even with the best intentions, maintaining inspiration can sometimes pose a challenge, particularly when faced with the monotony of daily tasks. Here are some strategies to keep the fires of inspiration burning:

1. Celebrating Wins

Regularly celebrate your accomplishments to stay motivated. Recognizing both small and big achievements creates a positive feedback loop that reinvigorates your ambition. Whether you take yourself out for a nice dinner, share your success with your accountability partner, or treat your team to a team-building event, acknowledging progress is essential for sustaining motivation.

2. Creating a Vision Board

A vision board is a powerful visual representation of your goals and aspirations. By curating images, quotes, and other motivational elements that resonate with your vision, you create a source of inspiration that serves as a constant reminder of your ultimate objectives. Place your vision board where you can see it daily; it serves as a compelling motivator, helping you maintain focus even during routine tasks.

3. **Staying Connected to Your Purpose**

Regularly revisit your 'why'—the underlying purpose that drives your entrepreneurial ambitions. What motivated you to start your business in the first place? Reflecting on your core values ensures you remain aligned with your passion and reminds you of the importance of the journey. When challenges arise, reconnecting with your purpose can reignite the fire that initially inspired you.

Conclusion: The Journey from Inspiration to Action

As we conclude this chapter, it is clear that the transformation from inspiration to action is a fundamental aspect of entrepreneurship. While inspiration may ignite the spark, it is disciplined action and accountability that fuel the fire, propelling you forward on your journey to success.

Embrace the mindset of an action-oriented entrepreneur. Utilize the tools and techniques discussed in this chapter to cultivate a habit of translating your inspired ideas into tangible results. Establish an accountability framework that keeps you honest and committed while surrounding yourself with the motivational influences that will drive you onward.

Remember that the entrepreneurial landscape is filled with opportunities, but it is up to you to seize them. By transforming inspiration into action, you not only position yourself for success but also inspire those around you to do the same. Your journey is a testament to the power of turning ideas into reality, and with each step you take, you uncover new possibilities for innovation, growth, and impact.

As you continue your adventurous journey, let inspiration be the fuel that guides you, while action becomes the vehicle that takes you to your destination. The world awaits the unique contributions only you can make—so take that leap, embrace action, and watch your entrepreneurial aspirations come to life!

Reflection

Take a moment to write down a recent moment of inspiration that you experienced. What actions can you identify that will help transform this inspiration into reality? Break it down into achievable steps and set a timeline. Commit to taking the first step today, and remember, every great journey begins with a single action.

Chapter 4

The Art of Discipline

The vital role of discipline in bridging dreams and reality.

Discipline is the backbone of success in entrepreneurship. It is the practice of training oneself to adhere to a set of standards, rules, or principles consistently. While inspiration can ignite the entrepreneurial spirit, it is discipline that sustains momentum, drives productivity, and ultimately transforms ideas into reality. In this chapter, we will explore the importance of discipline, how to cultivate it, and the ways it impacts your journey as an entrepreneur.

The Importance of Discipline

Discipline is more than merely adhering to schedules and routines; it is a comprehensive approach to achieving goals. For entrepreneurs, discipline plays a pivotal role in several key areas:

1. **Consistency**: Building a successful business requires consistent effort. Discipline ensures that you show up every day, working toward your goals, even when motivation wanes or obstacles arise. It is this consistent approach that leads to gradual progress, ultimately resulting in significant achievements.

2. **Time Management**: Entrepreneurs often juggle multiple responsibilities, from managing finances to developing new products. Discipline helps you prioritize tasks and manage your time effectively,

allowing you to focus on high-impact activities that drive your business forward.

3. **Goal Achievement**: Discipline is essential for setting and achieving both short-term and long-term goals. By committing to a structured approach, you can break down larger ambitions into manageable tasks and ensure that all necessary steps are taken to reach your desired outcomes.

Cultivating Discipline

1. **Establish Morning Routines**

Your morning routine sets the tone for the day. Developing a consistent morning practice can help you cultivate discipline by preparing you mentally and physically for the day ahead. Consider incorporating activities such as exercise, meditation, reading, or journaling into your morning routine. These practices not only promote well-being but also instill a sense of structure in your day.

For example, if you set a goal to write a certain number of pages for a project each day, designate a specific time in your morning routine for writing. By making it a non-negotiable part of your day, you create a disciplined habit that fosters focus and creativity.

2. **Create SMART Goals**

Setting SMART (Specific, Measurable, Achievable, Relevant, and Time-bound) goals is a powerful way to cultivate discipline. By clarifying precisely what you want to achieve and outlining the steps needed to get there, you create a roadmap that guides your daily actions.

For instance, instead of saying, "I want to grow my business," a SMART goal would be, "I want to increase my customer base by 20% over the next six months by implementing a targeted social media marketing strategy." This goal provides a clear direction and timeline, making it easier to remain disciplined in taking necessary actions.

3. **Accountability Measures**

Implementing accountability measures is one of the most effective ways to cultivate discipline. Share your goals with a mentor, business partner, or accountability group to encourage commitment and support. Regular check-ins with an accountability partner can help keep you focused and motivated, providing an external incentive to follow through on your plans.

Additionally, consider rewarding yourself for achieving milestones. Celebrating your progress acknowledges your efforts and reinforces disciplined behavior, creating a positive feedback loop.

4. **Embrace Routine and Structure**

Establishing a daily routine that includes specific times for work, breaks, and self-care can significantly enhance your discipline. Structure provides a framework within which you can thrive. Identify the most productive hours of your day and allocate them to high-priority tasks.

For example, if you find that you work best in the early morning, reserve that time for your most challenging projects. By creating a clear structure, you reduce the chances of procrastination and distraction, allowing discipline to flourish.

Overcoming Challenges to Discipline

Even with the best intentions, maintaining discipline can be challenging. Here are some strategies to overcome common obstacles:

1. **Combat Procrastination**

Procrastination is perhaps the greatest enemy of discipline. When faced with daunting tasks, it's easy to put them off for another day. Combat procrastination by breaking down larger projects into smaller, more manageable tasks. The act of starting—even if it's just a few minutes—can create momentum and diminish feelings of overwhelm.

2. **Manage Distractions**

In today's fast-paced world, distractions abound. Social media, notifications, and multitasking can derail your focus and undermine your discipline. Identify your key distractions and develop strategies to minimize them. For example, designate specific times for checking emails and social media, and consider using apps that block distracting websites during work hours.

3. **Practice Self-Compassion**

Discipline does not mean rigidity; rather, it is about progress and growth. If you encounter setbacks or fail to meet your own expectations, practice self-compassion. Acknowledge that setbacks are a natural part of the entrepreneurial journey, and use them as opportunities for learning and reflection.

Instead of berating yourself for missed deadlines, ask, "What can I learn from this experience?" Adopting a self-compassionate mindset can help.

Adopting a self-compassionate mindset can help reduce feelings of guilt or failure, allowing you to refocus your energy on constructive actions. Rather than dwelling on your shortcomings, treat each setback as a learning opportunity. This shift in perspective reinforces resilience and encourages you to maintain discipline in the face of adversity.

The Long-Term Impact of Discipline

Discipline is not merely a short-term strategy; it is a way of life that has long-lasting effects on your personal and professional growth. As you cultivate discipline, you cultivate character, setting the stage for future successes. Here are a few key areas in which discipline can positively impact your entrepreneurial journey:

1. **Building Confidence**: As you consistently take action towards your goals, you create a tangible track record of achievements, regardless of their size. This accumulation of successes fosters self-confidence and reinforces your ability to handle challenges. Each step taken reinforces the belief that you have the power to achieve your ambitions.

2. **Developing Resilience**: Entrepreneurs face a myriad of challenges, from market fluctuations to unexpected hurdles. Discipline cultivates resilience, enabling you

to adapt and bounce back when faced with difficulties. This resilience can set you apart in a competitive landscape, helping you navigate uncertainties with an unwavering mindset.

3. **Creating a Legacy**: Ultimately, the disciplined actions you take today will pave the way for the legacy you leave behind. As you consistently demonstrate integrity, commitment, and excellence in your endeavors, you inspire others to do the same. Your disciplined approach to entrepreneurship can influence the culture of your organization and the community you serve, creating a ripple effect that inspires others to pursue their passions with dedication.

As we conclude this chapter on the art of discipline, it's essential to recognize that while discipline is crucial for success, it should not come at the expense of creativity and adaptability. The most successful entrepreneurs understand the delicate balance between maintaining structure and allowing for flexibility.

Cultivating discipline doesn't mean you must rigidly adhere to a predetermined plan. Instead, it means committing to a process that puts you in the best position to succeed. Embrace the concept of disciplined flexibility—remaining dedicated to your goals, while also being open to adjusting your path as new information and opportunities arise.

As you embark on your entrepreneurial journey, remember that discipline is your ally. It is the steady hand that guides you through the unpredictability of business. With a strong foundation of discipline, you can turn inspiration into actionable strategies that lead to meaningful achievements.

Reflect on the discipline you wish to cultivate. Identify areas where you could strengthen your approach, and take actionable steps to create lasting habits that propel your success. With each small victory, you build the disciplined mindset needed to navigate the entrepreneurial landscape and achieve your dreams.

Reflection

Take a moment to reflect on your own discipline practices. In which areas do you excel, and where could you improve? Write down one specific action you can take this week to strengthen your discipline. Whether it's establishing a new routine, setting SMART goals, or seeking an accountability partner, commit to that action and embrace the transformative power of discipline in your entrepreneurial journey.

Chapter 5

Think Differently

Innovative thinking and challenging the status quo.

In the fast-paced world of entrepreneurship, conventional wisdom can often stifle innovation and creativity. The ability to think differently—to approach problems from unique angles and challenge the status quo—is not just a valuable skill; it is essential for survival and growth in today's competitive landscape. In this chapter, we will explore the concept of thinking differently, its significance in entrepreneurship, and practical strategies to cultivate innovative thinking.

The Case for Thinking Differently

Thinking differently is about adopting a mindset that embraces innovation, risks unconventional paths, and remains open to new ideas. It begins with the recognition that traditional solutions may not yield the best outcomes in an ever-changing marketplace. This mindset empowers entrepreneurs to unravel complexities in their industries and discover unexplored opportunities.

Several iconic entrepreneurs and thinkers have demonstrated the power of unconventional thinking in their success stories. Consider Steve Jobs, who revolutionized the tech industry by focusing not just on functionality but on design and user experience. By thinking differently, he transformed Apple into a brand synonymous with creativity and innovation.

The Role of Creativity in Entrepreneurship

Creativity is the cornerstone of innovative thinking. It is the process of generating original ideas and solutions that drive change and improvement. Entrepreneurs who embrace creativity can differentiate their products, services, and approaches, resulting in a competitive advantage.

1. Breaking Free from Constraints

One of the primary obstacles to creative thinking is the fear of failure and constraints imposed by existing norms. Entrepreneurs often feel pressured to conform to industry standards or best practices, inhibiting their ability to think outside the box. To cultivate creativity, it is essential to break free from these constraints and encourage a culture of experimentation.

Create an environment where ideas can be explored without judgment. Encourage team members to share their thoughts and propose unconventional solutions, even if they initially seem implausible. This approach fosters a culture of creativity where innovation thrives.

2. Diverse Perspectives

Incorporating diverse perspectives into the creative process enhances the quality of ideas and solutions. Surrounding yourself with individuals from various backgrounds, experiences, and disciplines broadens the spectrum of ideas available. Diverse teams are proven to generate more innovative solutions compared to homogeneous groups.

Engaging in discussions with people who think differently can stimulate fresh ideas. Seek out mentors and peers from different industries or fields, attend networking events, and participate in forums that expose you to varied viewpoints. By embracing diversity, you create opportunities for innovative thinking.

Strategies to Enhance Your Ability to Think Differently

1. Question Assumptions

To think differently, entrepreneurs must actively challenge assumptions—both their own and those ingrained in their industry. Often, we accept certain beliefs as given, leading to a narrow approach to problem-solving. Ask yourself questions like:

- What do I assume to be true about my industry?

- Are there alternative perspectives I haven't considered?

- What if the opposite were true?

By questioning long-held beliefs, you can identify new pathways to explore. This reflective practice encourages creativity and opens the door to innovative solutions.

2. Adopt a "Fail Fast" Mindset

Innovation often involves trial and error. Embrace a mindset that encourages trial, experimentation, and even failure as a necessary component of the creative process. By adopting a "fail fast" approach, you can quickly learn from missteps, adjust your course, and pivot toward more promising solutions.

Encourage your team to experiment with new ideas and initiatives without fear of failure. This approach promotes agility and allows you to seize opportunities as they arise.

3. **Engage in Creative Exercises**

Incorporate creative exercises into your routine to stimulate innovative thinking. Consider activities such as:

- **Brainstorming Sessions**: Gather your team for unstructured brainstorming sessions where no idea is too far-fetched. The goal is to generate a large volume of ideas and unleash creative thinking.

- **Mind Mapping**: Use mind mapping techniques to visually organize thoughts and connections related to a particular topic. This technique helps clarify ideas and reveals new avenues for exploration.

- **Design Thinking**: Implement design thinking principles to understand customer needs deeply and develop human-centered solutions. This iterative approach fosters creativity by empathizing with users and prototyping ideas rapidly.

The Power of Open-Mindedness

Open-mindedness is a key trait of innovative thinkers. Embracing diverse perspectives and being receptive to new ideas is vital for cultivating creativity. Challenge yourself to seek out ideas that seem contrary to your beliefs or experiences.

1. **Seek Feedback**

Encourage constructive feedback on your ideas from peers, mentors, and even customers. This feedback can provide valuable insights and highlight blind spots that may impede your creative thinking. Being open to differing viewpoints enriches your understanding and can lead to breakthroughs.

2. **Practice Active Listening**

Engage in active listening during conversations. Rather than formulating a response while the other person is speaking, focus entirely on understanding their perspective. This practice encourages deeper discussions and fosters an environment of collaboration, prompting innovative ideas to surface.

Embrace Continuous Learning

Innovation is a moving target, and staying relevant requires a commitment to continuous learning. The best entrepreneurs understand that knowledge is not static; it evolves as new technologies, trends, and consumer preferences emerge. To think differently, you must cultivate a mindset that welcomes learning opportunities—both formal and informal.

1. **Engage in Professional Development**

Take advantage of workshops, online courses, and seminars within your industry or related fields. Expanding your knowledge base allows you to acquire new skills and insights that can fuel creativity. Look for opportunities to learn from industry leaders and innovative thinkers, as their experiences often provide invaluable lessons.

2. **Read Widely and Diversely**

Reading is one of the easiest ways to expose yourself to new ideas and concepts. Read books, articles, and journals across various subjects—not only those directly related to your business. Delving into philosophy, psychology, art, and technology can introduce new frameworks for thinking, inspiring innovative approaches in your entrepreneurial endeavors.

3. **Network Strategically**

Networking is more than just a means of building relationships; it's an opportunity to learn from others and exchange ideas. Attend industry conferences, join professional organizations, and participate in networking events to connect with like-minded individuals. Engaging in meaningful conversations with individuals outside of your immediate domain can lead to new ideas and collaborations that foster innovative thinking.

Taking Action on New Ideas

Thinking differently is not just about generating ideas; it necessitates the courage to take action. Once you've identified innovative solutions or creative concepts, you must implement them to see results.

1. **Create an Action Plan**

Turning ideas into reality requires a well-thought-out action plan. Outline the steps necessary to implement your new concept, target resources needed, assign responsibilities, and set timelines. A clear plan will guide your team and help ensure accountability.

2. **Pilot and Test**

Before fully deploying a new idea, consider running a pilot program or test phase. This approach allows you to assess the viability and effectiveness of your concept in a controlled environment. Gather feedback from participants and analyze the results to make any necessary adjustments before the full launch.

3. **Learn from Outcomes**

Regardless of the outcome—success or failure—it's critical to evaluate the results of each new idea you implement. Reflect on what worked well, what didn't, and why. This reflective practice informs future decisions and enhances your ability to think differently in subsequent endeavors.

As we conclude this chapter on thinking differently, remember that the journey of innovation is ongoing. By committing to an innovative mindset and embracing the principles outlined in this chapter, you empower yourself to break free from convention, uncover new opportunities, and create meaningful solutions.

Thinking differently is not just a skill; it's a way of life that fosters resilience and adaptability. It challenges you to rise above the ordinary and redefine what's possible. By cultivating creativity, embracing diverse perspectives, and maintaining an open-minded approach, you can lead your business to new heights.

As you move forward in your entrepreneurial journey, carry with you the understanding that innovation takes time, effort, and courage. Embrace experimentation, learn from experiences, and remain committed to walking the uncharted path. With a mindset rooted in thinking differently, you have the potential to make a significant impact on your industry and inspire others to do the same.

Reflection

Take a moment to reflect on your current approach to thinking and creativity. What are some areas where you have felt constrained by convention? Identify one new idea or perspective you have been considering. Write down an actionable step you can take this week to explore that idea further—whether it's conducting research, discussing it with someone, or testing it on a small scale. Embrace the power of thinking differently and let it guide you toward innovative opportunities.

Chapter 6

The Ripple Effect of Influence

How your presence and actions impact others and your community.

In the realm of entrepreneurship, influence is more than just a tool for persuasion; it is a profound force that shapes not only individual interactions but also entire communities and industries. Every entrepreneur has the ability to create a ripple effect—an impact that extends far beyond their immediate sphere of influence. In this chapter, we will explore the concept of influence, how it manifests in everyday actions, and the importance of harnessing this power to create a positive ripple effect in your community and beyond.

Understanding Influence

At its core, influence is the capacity to have an effect on the character, development, or behavior of someone or something. As entrepreneurs, our influence can manifest in countless ways, from the products we create to the relationships we cultivate. Our presence speaks volumes; how we conduct ourselves; the values we embody, and the decisions we make can inspire others to think, act, and even change their own behaviors.

1. **Personal Influence**: As individuals, we wield personal influence through our actions, words, and interactions. This influence is grounded in authenticity, integrity, and consistent behavior. When

others perceive us as trustworthy and genuine, our ability to influence them grows significantly.

2. **Organizational Influence**: Businesses as organizations also have a collective influence on their industry and customers. The values, mission, and practices of a company shape its reputation and can inspire loyalty among customers and employees alike. A business that embodies social responsibility or ethical practices can encourage others in the industry to follow suit.

The Ripple Effect in Action

The ripple effect of influence can be seen in various contexts—personal relationships, professional networks, community actions, and even global movements. When you impart positive influence, you create a ripple that can inspire numerous others to take action. Here are some examples of the ripple effect at work:

1. **Inspiring Innovation**: As an entrepreneur, your innovative ideas can inspire others to think creatively and pursue their ambitious projects. Consider an entrepreneur who develops a groundbreaking technology. Their success can encourage aspiring tech innovators, leading to a wave of new inventions and advancements in the field—creating a cycle of inspiration and innovation.

2. **Community Engagement**: By actively participating in your community and supporting local initiatives, you not only contribute to social good but also motivate others to do the same. For instance, if you lead a small business that sponsors local events or charities, you set an example that can inspire others in your

community to become more involved. Your actions create a culture of giving and togetherness that can lead to collective improvement.

3. **Mentorship and Leadership**: As a successful entrepreneur, you have the opportunity to mentor others and share your experiences. This influence can empower individuals to pursue their ambitions and overcome obstacles. When you mentor someone, you instill confidence and provide guidance, creating a ripple effect as they, in turn, mentor others in their journey.

The Power of Authenticity

The effectiveness of your influence stems from authenticity. In a world saturated with information and noise, people gravitate toward authenticity—individuals who genuinely embody their values and beliefs. Authenticity cultivates trust, which is fundamental to influence.

1. **Lead by Example**: Your actions must align with your stated values. If you advocate for sustainability in your business, ensure that your practices reflect this commitment. By consistently demonstrating your values, you gain credibility and inspire others to do the same.

2. **Share Vulnerabilities**: Transparency about your challenges and failures allows you to connect on a deeper level with others. Sharing your journey, including struggles, helps people see the human side of entrepreneurship. This vulnerability fosters relatability and makes your influence more impactful.

Strategies to Enhance Your Influence

1. **Build Strong Relationships**

Influence thrives in relationships. Take the time to build meaningful connections with others, whether they are team members, clients, or fellow entrepreneurs. Genuine relationships create a foundation for trust and open communication, allowing your influence to be more effective.

- **Networking**: Attend industry events and engage with peers across various platforms. Be open to collaborations, partnerships, and discussions that can lead to a mutually beneficial exchange of ideas and support.

2. **Communicate Effectively**

Effective communication is critical for influence. Articulate your ideas, vision, and values clearly. Engaging storytelling can captivate audiences and inspire action.

- **Emotional Intelligence**: Cultivating emotional intelligence allows you to understand and empathize with others. By communicating in a way that resonates emotionally, you strengthen your influence and develop deeper connections with your audience.

3. **Champion Causes**

Utilize your influence to advocate for causes that resonate with you and your community. Whether it's supporting environmental sustainability, promoting diversity and inclusion, or championing social justice, align your efforts with meaningful initiatives that inspire change.

By embracing a cause and actively supporting it, you amplify your influence and mobilize others to join the movement. This can lead to a collective impact that extends far beyond your individual actions.

The Long-Term Benefits of Positive Influence

Influencing others for the better cultivates a legacy that lasts well beyond your immediate actions. The long-term benefits of creating a positive ripple effect extend not only to those you inspire but also to your business and community. Here are some of the key benefits associated with positive influence:

1. Cultivating a Supportive Community

By fostering positive influence, you contribute to building a community characterized by collaboration, support, and shared values. When individuals within a community see the positive impact of their actions, they are motivated to engage further. This cycle can create an environment where people uplift one another, share resources, and work collectively toward common goals, leading to sustainable growth and improvement.

2. Strengthening Brand Loyalty

A business that champions ethical practices, social responsibility, and positive influence attracts loyal customers who share similar values. When your influence aligns with your brand's mission, customers become not just consumers but advocates. They feel a sense of connection to your brand and are more likely to recommend it to others, enhancing your reputation and expanding your reach.

3. Inspiring Future Generations

The ripple effect of your influence can shape the values and aspirations of future generations. By setting a positive example, you inspire young entrepreneurs and thinkers to embrace innovation, integrity, and community engagement. As they grow, they carry forward the lessons learned from your actions, perpetuating a cycle of positive influence that can lead to transformative change in society.

As we conclude this chapter, it's important to recognize that with the power of influence comes responsibility. Being aware of how your presence and actions impact others equips you to make conscious choices that foster positivity and inspiration. Embrace the notion that your influence matters—every interaction, every decision, and every moment contributes to the larger tapestry of your community and industry.

As an entrepreneur, you have the potential to be a beacon of influence, guiding others toward excellence and integrity. By leading with authenticity, cultivating meaningful relationships, and championing causes that inspire you, you create a ripple effect that resonates far beyond your immediate circle.

Reflect on the legacy you wish to create through your influence. What are the values you want to impart? How do you want to be remembered in your community and industry? Take actionable steps to harness your influence for good, thereby creating a positive impact that inspires others to follow your lead.

Reflection

Consider the ways in which you currently influence those around you. Who are the people you admire for their positive influence? What specific actions or qualities do they embody that resonate with you? Write down one commitment you can make today to increase your positive influence within your community or network. Whether it's mentoring someone, advocating for a cause, or simply being more mindful of your interactions with others, every small effort contributes to the larger ripple effect of influence.

Chapter 7

Collab and Conquer

The power of strategic partnerships and collaborations.

In the dynamic world of entrepreneurship, one principle rings true: collaboration is often the key to success. No entrepreneur exists in a vacuum; every individual is part of a larger community that includes customers, partners, mentors, and even competitors. Harnessing the power of strategic partnerships and collaborations can drive innovation, enhance growth, and unlock new opportunities. In this chapter, we will explore the significance of collaboration, various types of partnerships, and actionable strategies for fostering fruitful collaborations.

The Significance of Collaboration

Collaboration is the process of working together with others to achieve a common purpose or result. When entrepreneurs collaborate, they can pool resources, share expertise, and leverage each other's strengths, leading to enhanced creativity and innovation. Here are several reasons why collaboration is essential in entrepreneurship:

1. **Expanding Reach and Audience**: Collaborative efforts can significantly amplify your reach. By joining forces with another entrepreneur, you tap into their audience and vice versa. This mutual sharing facilitates increased visibility and opens doors to new markets that may have been previously inaccessible.

2. **Diverse Skill Sets**: Collaborating with others who possess complementary skills allows you to combine talents and expertise. For instance, a tech

entrepreneur may partner with a marketing expert to ensure that their product not only functions effectively but is also well-promoted. This combination of skills increases the likelihood of success.

3. **Innovation Through Diverse Perspectives**: Collaboration fosters an environment that encourages the exchange of ideas. When individuals from different backgrounds work together, they bring unique perspectives and diverse approaches to problem-solving. This diversity can spark new ideas and lead to innovative solutions that wouldn't have been possible in isolation.

4. **Risk Mitigation**: Entrepreneurship is inherently risky, and collaboration can help mitigate some of that risk. When entrepreneurs pool resources and share responsibilities, they can alleviate the burden on any one individual and create a safety net that supports experimentation and growth.

Types of Partnerships and Collaborations

Understanding the various types of partnerships available can help entrepreneurs identify the most effective collaborations for their specific needs. Here are some common types of collaborations:

1. **Joint Ventures**: A joint venture involves two or more parties coming together to undertake a specific project or business activity. Each party contributes resources, shares risks, and collaborates on the

management of the project. This type of partnership is ideal for large-scale projects or entering new markets.

2. **Strategic Alliances**: Strategic alliances are non-equity partnerships that allow companies to collaborate while maintaining their independence. These alliances can involve co-marketing efforts, sharing distribution channels, or collaborating on research and development. Strategic alliances are flexible and can vary widely in scope.

3. **Co-Branding**: Co-branding occurs when two or more brands collaborate on a product or service, leveraging each other's reputations and audiences. This approach can enhance brand perception and create unique offerings. For example, a well-known food brand partnering with a celebrity chef to create exclusive recipes can yield substantial marketing benefits for both parties.

4. **Mentorship and Support Networks**: Collaborating with mentors and industry peers creates a supportive network that fosters growth and resilience. Engaging with experienced entrepreneurs allows you to learn from their insights, navigate challenges, and gain guidance as you develop your business.

5. **Community Collaborations**: Local businesses can gain significant benefits from collaborating with each other and local organizations. By partnering for community events, workshops, or joint promotions, businesses can strengthen their ties to the community while driving traffic and interest.

Strategies for Building Effective Collaborations

1. **Identify Complementary Goals**

The foundation of any successful collaboration lies in shared goals and values. Before entering a partnership, take the time to clearly define what you hope to achieve and ensure alignment with potential partners. Establishing common objectives fosters trust and excitement while ensuring that all parties are working toward a mutually beneficial outcome.

2. **Communicate Openly and Clearly**

Effective communication is crucial for successful collaboration. Be transparent about your expectations, requirements, and limitations. Regular check-ins and updates help maintain transparency throughout the collaboration, allowing you to address any challenges as they arise. Open communication also fosters a sense of camaraderie and strengthens the partnership.

3. **Leverage Each Other's Strengths**

Recognize and appreciate the unique strengths that each party brings to the table. Clearly delineate roles and responsibilities to prevent confusion and ensure that each individual can contribute effectively. Create a collaborative environment where everyone feels valued and empowered to make meaningful contributions.

4. **Create Structured Agreements**

Define the terms of the collaboration early on. Whether it involves a joint venture or a simple co-marketing agreement, formalizing expectations, timelines, and responsibilities can prevent misunderstandings and pave the way for smooth execution. Ensure that all parties have a clear understanding of their commitments.

5. Build a Relationship Beyond Business

While business objectives are essential, strive to build genuine relationships with your collaborators. Take the time to understand their values, interests, and motivations. Nurturing a positive rapport can lead to a more fruitful collaboration and an environment of trust and mutual respect. Building personal connections can often lead to more successful outcomes as collaborators feel comfortable sharing ideas and providing constructive feedback.

Cultivating a Culture of Collaboration

1. Encourage a Collaborative Mindset

As an entrepreneur, fostering a culture of collaboration within your organization or among your peers is essential. Encourage your team members to think beyond their individual tasks and seek opportunities to work together. Celebrate team accomplishments and recognize collaborative efforts that lead to innovative solutions. When collaboration is part of your company culture, it becomes a natural and valuable practice.

2. Utilize Technology to Facilitate Collaboration

Leverage technology to enhance collaboration among partners, team members, and external stakeholders. Collaboration tools such as Slack, Microsoft Teams, or project management platforms like Trello and Asana can help streamline communication and project tracking. These tools facilitate real-time collaboration, making it easier to share ideas, provide feedback, and ensure everyone stays aligned on objectives and deadlines.

3. **Gather Feedback and Reflect**

After a collaboration concludes, take the time to reflect on the experience. Gather feedback from all parties involved to assess what worked well and what could be improved in future collaborations. This practice allows you to learn from each partnership, refine processes, and build stronger collaborations moving forward.

The Long-Term Impact of Collaboration

The benefits of collaboration extend well beyond immediate gains. By fostering partnerships and collaborations, entrepreneurs can create a legacy of innovation, support, and growth within their industries and communities. Here are some long-term impacts of effective collaboration:

1. **Shared Learning and Development**: Collaborative efforts often open the door to shared learning opportunities. Partners can learn from each other's successes and mistakes, enhancing their skills and knowledge. This continuous development allows businesses to adapt more quickly to changing landscapes and consumer demands.

2. **Increased Resilience**: In difficult times, collaborative partnerships can act as a support system. Businesses working together can navigate challenges more effectively by pooling resources, sharing information, and problem-solving collectively. This resilience can make all parties involved stronger and more capable of overcoming adversity.

3. **Fostering Innovation Across Industries**: By collaborating across different industries, entrepreneurs can drive innovation and creativity in new ways. Cross-industry partnerships can lead to groundbreaking ideas and solutions that benefit not just the partners involved, but also consumers and communities at large.

4. **Sustaining Community Engagement**: Engaging with local businesses and organizations helps create a sense of connection and community. Entrepreneurs who prioritize collaboration contribute to a thriving local economy and drive social change by uplifting one another and working together on community initiatives.

As we wrap up this chapter on collaboration, it is essential to recognize that the biggest successes in entrepreneurship are rarely achieved in isolation. The connections you forge and the partnerships you cultivate can propel your business forward in ways that would be impossible alone.

The power of collaboration lies not only in achieving distinct business objectives but also in creating a network of influence, support, and innovation. Embrace the mindset of collaboration, actively seek out strategic partnerships, and commit to building relationships that yield mutual benefits.

Remember that every interaction counts, and your willingness to collaborate can create a ripple effect that impacts individuals and communities for generations. As you venture forward in your entrepreneurial journey, let the mantra "collab and conquer" guide you. Together, we can achieve more, inspire innovation, and transform the entrepreneurial landscape.

Reflection

Take a moment to identify potential collaborators in your network. Who shares similar values or complements your strengths? Write down a list of individuals or organizations you would like to explore partnerships with. Consider what type of collaboration would be most beneficial for both parties. Develop an actionable plan for reaching out to one of these potential collaborations. By taking decisive steps, you'll unlock new opportunities and strengthen your foothold as an influential entrepreneur.

Chapter 8

High-Performance Mindset

Techniques for boosting performance and productivity.

In the fast-paced world of entrepreneurship, the distinction between success and mediocrity often lies in the mindset of the individual. A high-performance mindset is characterized by an unwavering commitment to excellence, resilience in the face of challenges, and a proactive approach to growth and development. This chapter will explore the foundations of a high-performance mindset, techniques to boost your performance and productivity, and the practices that can help you maintain this mindset in your entrepreneurial journey.

The Foundations of a High-Performance Mindset

A high-performance mindset is built upon several core principles that empower entrepreneurs to achieve their goals and realize their full potential:

1. **Growth Orientation**: At the heart of a high-performance mindset is the belief that abilities and intelligence can be developed through dedication and effort. This growth-oriented perspective helps entrepreneurs embrace challenges, persist in the face of setbacks, and view failures as opportunities for learning. By adopting a mindset focused on growth, you remain open to new experiences, ideas, and skills.

2. **Resilience**: The ability to bounce back from adversity is a hallmark of high performers. Resilience not only helps you navigate setbacks but also enables you to adapt to evolving circumstances. By cultivating

resilience, you build the capacity to stay focused on your goals and maintain motivation, even during difficult times.

3. **Clarity of Purpose**: A high-performance mindset is driven by a clear sense of purpose. Understanding your "why" provides motivation and direction for your actions. When you align your goals with your deeper values and passions, your commitment to high performance intensifies, and your actions become more purposeful.

Techniques for Boosting Performance

1. Set SMART Goals

Establishing clear, specific, measurable, achievable, relevant, and time-bound (SMART) goals is fundamental to enhancing performance. Breaking down larger goals into smaller, actionable steps allows you to focus on immediate tasks while maintaining an awareness of your overall objectives. This approach helps you avoid feeling overwhelmed, fostering sustained motivation and momentum.

2. Practice Time Management

Effective time management is crucial for maximizing productivity. Adopting techniques such as the Pomodoro Technique—where you work in focused intervals followed by short breaks—can help maintain concentration and prevent burnout. Prioritize tasks based on urgency and importance, using tools like the Eisenhower Matrix to clarify what requires immediate attention and what can be delegated or deferred.

3. Establish Routines

Creating daily routines fosters structure and consistency, enabling high levels of performance. Routines help you streamline processes, reduce decision fatigue, and carve out time for essential activities. Consider incorporating a morning ritual that includes exercise, goal-setting, or mindfulness practices to kickstart your day with energy and focus.

4. Eliminate Distractions

Identifying and mitigating distractions is key to optimizing productivity. Take stock of potential interruptions, such as notifications from devices, social media, or noisy environments. Designate specific times for checking emails and messages, and create a dedicated workspace that minimizes external distractions. This intentional approach enhances your ability to concentrate and perform at a high level.

5. Leverage Technology

Utilizing productivity tools and software can aid in streamlining tasks and enhancing performance. Consider employing project management tools like Asana or Trello to track progress and collaborate efficiently. Calendar applications can help manage your schedule and set reminders for important deadlines. By leveraging technology effectively, you can focus on critical tasks and maximize productivity.

Cultivating a High-Performance Environment

1. Surround Yourself with Excellence

The people you choose to associate with play a significant role in shaping your mindset. Seek to surround yourself with high-performing individuals who inspire and motivate you to elevate your standards. Engaging with a community of ambitious entrepreneurs encourages accountability and offers opportunities for collaboration and mentorship.

2. Foster a Growth Culture

If you lead a team, prioritize creating a culture of growth and excellence within your organization. Encourage open communication and provide opportunities for development and learning. Acknowledge and celebrate successes to reinforce a positive culture that nurtures high performance.

3. Provide Constructive Feedback

Feedback is essential for improvement and growth. Encourage a feedback-rich environment where team members can provide insights and suggestions for improvement. Constructive feedback supports continuous learning, allowing everyone to enhance their performance and contribute more effectively to shared goals.

Maintaining a High-Performance Mindset

1. Practice Mindfulness and Reflection

In the hustle and bustle of entrepreneurship, it's important to take moments for mindfulness and self-reflection. Mindfulness practices such as meditation, journaling, or deep breathing can help ground your thoughts and emotions, enhancing clarity and focus. Regularly reflecting on your progress and experiences allows you to reevaluate your goals and adjust your approach as necessary.

2. Stay Physically Active

Physical well-being is intricately linked to mental performance. Regular exercise boosts energy levels, reduces stress, and improves cognitive function. Incorporate physical activity into your daily routine—whether through high-intensity workouts, walking, or yoga—to maintain optimal health and performance.

3. Prioritize Mental Well-Being

In addition to physical health, maintaining your mental well-being is crucial for sustaining a high-performance mindset. Stress management techniques, such as mindfulness meditation or relaxation exercises, can help mitigate anxiety and promote a sense of calm. Furthermore, ensuring you have adequate sleep and a balanced diet provides the foundation needed for optimal cognitive function and resilience.

4. Continuous Learning and Adaptation

A high-performance mindset thrives on continuous learning. Stay curious and committed to improving your skills and knowledge. Regularly invest time in professional development—through workshops, online courses, or reading—so you can stay ahead in your field and adapt to changes effectively. Embrace feedback from others as a valuable tool for growth, as it offers insights that can refine your approach.

The Long-Term Benefits of a High-Performance Mindset

1. **Enhanced Achievement**: Cultivating a high-performance mindset leads to greater achievement over time. By setting and consistently pursuing

ambitious goals, you position yourself for success and create a pattern of accomplishment that fuels future aspirations.

2. **Greater Resilience**: A mindset focused on high performance instills resilience. You develop the mental fortitude necessary to overcome obstacles, learn from your mistakes, and persevere through challenges.

3. **Sustained Motivation**: Clarity of purpose and continuous self-improvement keep your motivation high. As you see progress and develop new skills, your enthusiasm for your work and your mission will continue to grow.

4. **Positive Influence on Others**: A high-performance mindset often inspires those around you. By embodying excellence and commitment, you influence colleagues, employees, and peers to adopt similar standards, leading to a collective elevation in performance and productivity.

As we conclude this chapter on cultivating a high-performance mindset, remember that this journey is ongoing and dynamic. It requires conscious effort, regular reflection, and a commitment to self-improvement. By adopting the techniques discussed, you empower yourself to reach new heights in your entrepreneurial pursuits.

Engage with your goals passionately, surround yourself with a supportive network, and take proactive steps to enhance your performance and productivity. Embrace challenges as opportunities for growth, and maintain an unwavering belief in your ability to achieve excellence.

As you move forward in your entrepreneurial journey, let the principles of a high-performance mindset guide you. Aim not only to achieve your personal and professional goals but also to inspire those around you to elevate their performance. By doing so, you contribute to a culture of excellence that can transform your organization and community.

Reflection

Take a moment to evaluate your current performance and mindset. What areas do you believe you can improve upon to achieve a higher level of performance? Write down one specific action you will take in the coming week to enhance your productivity or develop your skills. Whether it's setting a new goal, implementing a time management strategy, or investing in your well-being, commit to this action and embrace the journey toward high performance.

Chapter 9

Turning Adversity into Advantage

Learning to thrive in challenging situations.

In the world of entrepreneurship, adversity is an inevitable companion. Challenges, setbacks, and obstacles are part and parcel of the entrepreneurial journey. However, the most successful entrepreneurs do not merely endure adversity; they learn to turn it into an advantage. This chapter will explore the mindset required to embrace challenges, techniques for navigating difficulties, and strategies to transform adversity into growth opportunities.

The Reality of Adversity in Entrepreneurship

Every entrepreneur has experienced adversity in some form, whether it be market fluctuations, financial setbacks, operational difficulties, or personal hurdles. While these experiences can be disheartening, they serve a crucial purpose: they test your resolve and reveal your true potential. The ability to respond positively to adversity distinguishes ordinary entrepreneurs from exceptional leaders.

1. **Reframing Challenges**: The first step in transforming adversity is reframing your perception of challenges. Instead of viewing them as insurmountable barriers, consider them opportunities for learning and growth. Adversity often forces you to re-evaluate your

approaches, strategies, and business practices. This process can lead to innovation, adaptability, and resilience.

2. **Acknowledging Emotions**: Facing adversity can evoke a range of emotions, including frustration, fear, and uncertainty. It's essential to acknowledge and process these emotions. Denying or suppressing feelings can lead to burnout and hinder your ability to respond effectively. Instead, allow yourself to feel, reflect, and then refocus on actionable steps forward.

Techniques for Navigating Adversity

1. Embrace a Growth Mindset

A growth mindset is the belief that skills, abilities, and intelligence can be developed through effort and perseverance. This mindset encourages you to embrace challenges as opportunities to improve rather than as obstacles to success. When faced with adversity, remind yourself of past challenges you've overcome. Each experience builds resilience and reinforces your capacity to adapt and grow.

2. Analyze the Situation

When adversity strikes, take a step back to analyze the situation objectively. Identify the root causes of the challenges you are facing. Are there external factors at play, or are there internal weaknesses that need to be addressed?

By conducting a thorough analysis, you can develop targeted solutions that directly address the issues at hand.

3. **Seek Support and Collaboration**

In times of adversity, reaching out for support is crucial. Don't hesitate to lean on colleagues, mentors, or your network for guidance. Engaging in discussions can lead to new perspectives, ideas, and strategies. Forming alliances with others facing similar challenges can also offer mutual support, fostering a sense of camaraderie as you navigate difficulties together.

4. **Maintain Flexibility and Adaptability**

The ability to pivot in response to adversity is a hallmark of successful entrepreneurs. While it's essential to have a plan in place, staying flexible allows you to adapt to changing circumstances. If a particular approach isn't yielding the desired results, be open to considering alternative strategies. This adaptability can often lead to unforeseen opportunities and innovations.

Transforming Adversity into Advantage

1. **Learning and Growth**

Adversity can serve as a powerful teacher. Each challenge carries lessons that can enhance your skills and knowledge. Make it a habit to reflect on challenging situations and extract valuable insights. Creating a learning journal can help you document these reflections and track your development over time. By continuously learning from adversity, you position yourself for future success.

2. Fostering Resilience

Resilience is the capacity to recover quickly from difficulties and bounce back stronger. Each time you navigate adversity, you build resilience that prepares you for future challenges. Embrace the belief that you can emerge from setbacks even stronger and more equipped to handle what lies ahead. This resilience not only enhances your performance but also instills confidence in those around you.

3. Innovation and Creativity

Adversity often breeds innovation. When faced with limitations, entrepreneurs are forced to think creatively and find alternative solutions. Use challenging situations as a catalyst for innovation. Brainstorm new ideas, explore different business models, or revamp existing processes. The necessity of adapting under pressure can lead to breakthroughs that may transform your business for the better.

4. Inspiring Others

Your response to adversity can have a far-reaching impact on others. When you demonstrate resilience, adaptability, and a positive attitude in challenging situations, you become a source of inspiration for employees, peers, and aspiring entrepreneurs. Share your experiences and lessons learned through adversity, showing others that challenges can be overcome and lead to positive outcomes.

Building a Culture of Resilience

1. Empower Your Team

As a leader, fostering a culture of resilience within your organization helps inspire others to embrace challenges. Encourage your team to view setbacks as opportunities for growth and innovation. Provide training, tools, and resources to equip them with the skills needed to navigate adversity effectively.

2. Create Open Channels of Communication

Encouraging open communication allows team members to share their concerns and challenges. Create an environment where employees feel safe discussing obstacles they are facing and brainstorming potential solutions together This collaborative approach enables the entire team to support one another during difficult times, fostering solidarity and collective problem-solving.

3. Celebrate Resilience

Recognizing and celebrating instances of resilience within your organization can reinforce the mindset that views adversity as a stepping stone to success. Acknowledge team members who have demonstrated tenacity and ingenuity during challenging projects or crises. By highlighting their contributions, you inspire a culture wherein overcoming difficulties is celebrated, motivating others to emulate similar behaviors.

As we conclude this chapter on turning adversity into advantage, it is important to remember that challenges are not the end of the road but rather detours that can lead to greater opportunities. The mindset you adopt in response to adversity will fundamentally shape your journey as an entrepreneur.

Adversity can serve as a powerful catalyst for personal and professional growth. By embracing challenges, learning from them, and fostering resilience both in yourself and within your team, you can transform setbacks into meaningful achievements.

Each time you encounter adversity, reflect on how far you've come and the lessons you've learned along the way. View challenges not as hindrances but as powerful opportunities to innovate, adapt, and grow stronger.

As you move forward in your entrepreneurial journey, take heart in the knowledge that adversity is an inherent part of the process. By mastering the art of turning challenges into advantages, you can not only enhance your own performance but also inspire others, create a resilient organization, and ultimately thrive in the face of adversity.

Reflection

Take a moment to reflect on a recent challenge you faced in your entrepreneurial journey. What lessons did you learn from that experience? Write down a specific action you can take in the future to turn adversity into an opportunity for growth. Whether it's seeking support, adjusting your strategy, or embracing a more resilient mindset, commit to implementing this action the next time you encounter challenges. Embrace adversity as a powerful teacher and a catalyst for your continued success.

Chapter 10

The Pivot Mindset

Strategies to pivot when necessary and embrace change.

In the ever-evolving landscape of entrepreneurship, the ability to pivot— to change direction in response to new information, market shifts, or unanticipated challenges—is crucial for sustained success. The Pivot Mindset involves recognizing when change is necessary and having the courage and flexibility to adapt your strategies accordingly. In this chapter, we will explore the importance of a pivot mindset, strategies for effectively pivoting when necessary, and real-world examples of entrepreneurs who embraced change to drive innovation and growth.

Understanding the Pivot Mindset

The concept of pivoting refers to making a fundamental change to your business strategy while keeping the overall vision intact. A pivot may involve altering your product or service, targeting a different customer segment, or even changing your business model. Adopting a pivot mindset means being open to change, viewing challenges as opportunities for growth, and maintaining a focus on long-term goals.

1. **Embracing Uncertainty**: Entrepreneurship is inherently uncertain. Market dynamics, consumer behavior, and economic conditions are continuously evolving. A pivot mindset allows you to embrace uncertainty instead of resisting it. By recognizing that change is a natural part of the entrepreneurial

journey, you equip yourself to respond proactively rather than reactively.

2. **Maintaining Customer Focus**: Successful pivots are often grounded in a deep understanding of customer needs and preferences. Keeping your customers at the center of your decision-making process ensures that your adaptations remain relevant and valuable. By listening to customer feedback, analyzing market trends, and observing competitive behaviors, you can make informed decisions about when and how to pivot.

Recognizing the Need to Pivot

The first step toward embracing the pivot mindset is recognizing when a shift is necessary. Here are some signs that it may be time to reconsider your approach:

1. **Declining Performance Indicators**: If you notice a consistent decline in sales, customer engagement, or market share, it may be a signal to reassess your strategy. Analyzing performance metrics can provide insights into areas that require change.

2. **Shifting Market Conditions**: Changes in market dynamics, such as the emergence of new competitors, evolving consumer preferences, or regulatory shifts, can necessitate a pivot. Staying attuned to external factors enables you to remain agile in the face of change.

3. **Customer Feedback and Insights**: Listening to your customers is vital. If you receive repeated feedback indicating that your product or service is not meeting

their needs, it's essential to take that feedback seriously. Customer insights can guide you toward meaningful pivots that enhance your value proposition.

4. **Internal Realignments**: Sometimes, a pivot is necessary due to changes within your organization— be it shifts in team capabilities, resources, or strategic direction. Assessing internal strengths and weaknesses can help identify areas where adjustments are needed.

Strategies for Effectively Pivoting

1. Conduct Thorough Market Research

Before making a pivot, conduct thorough market research to understand the landscape. This involves analyzing competitors, studying market trends, and gathering insights from existing customers. Data-driven decisions empower you to pivot in a direction that aligns with market demand and minimizes risks.

2. Establish a Prototype or Pilot Program

When considering a significant change, start small. Develop a prototype of your new product, service, or approach, and run a pilot program to test its viability. This iterative process allows you to gather valuable feedback without committing substantial resources upfront. Be prepared to refine and adjust based on the results of your pilot.

3. Communicate Changes Clearly

When implementing a pivot, clear communication is vital. Whether internally with your team or externally with customers and stakeholders, ensure that everyone understands the rationale behind the change. Highlight the benefits of the pivot and how it aligns with your overall vision. Effective communication fosters buy-in and encourages a smooth transition.

4. **Embrace Flexibility and Adaptability**

A successful pivot requires a willingness to be flexible and adapt to evolving circumstances. Stay open to feedback and remain agile throughout the transition. If initial changes do not yield the desired results, don't hesitate to iterate further based on new information.

5. **Leverage Your Network**

Utilize your network of mentors, peers, and industry contacts for support during the pivot process. Engage in conversations with others who have successfully navigated similar changes. Their insights and experiences can provide valuable guidance and perspective, helping you navigate your pivot effectively.

Real-World Examples of Successful Pivots

1. **Twitter**: Originally launched as a platform for podcasting called Odeo, the company faced challenges when Apple introduced its podcasting platform. In response to this setback, the team pivoted to a microblogging platform, resulting in the birth of Twitter—a now globally recognized social media platform focused on short-form content and real-time conversations.

2. **Netflix**: Netflix started as a DVD rental service but recognized the shift towards digital streaming. In the

early 2000s, the company made a strategic pivot to become a subscription-based streaming service, ultimately leading to its dominance in the entertainment industry. This strategic pivot allowed Netflix to leverage changing consumer behaviors and technological advancements, transforming it into a major player in content production and distribution.

3. **Instagram**: Instagram began as a check-in app called Burbn, which allowed users to check-in at locations and share photos. However, when the founders analyzed user interaction, they discovered that the photo-sharing feature was the most popular aspect of the app. Recognizing this opportunity, they pivoted to focus solely on photo-sharing, rebranding as Instagram, which quickly became a global phenomenon.

4. **Maintaining a Pivot Mindset for Long-Term Success**

5. **Continuous Learning**: Adopting a pivot mindset is not a one-time event; it is an ongoing practice. Continuously learn from your experiences, successes, and failures. Keep your ears open for industry trends and customer insights that may indicate the need for future pivots. Cultivating a culture of learning within your organization ensures that you remain responsive to change.

6. **Foster an Innovative Culture**: Encourage a culture of innovation and experimentation within your team. Providing opportunities for brainstorming and idea generation can lead to new solutions and approaches. When everyone feels empowered to contribute ideas,

you create a collective intelligence that can identify when a pivot is needed and develop creative strategies for implementation.

7. **Set a Regular Review Process**: Establish a routine for assessing your business performance, market conditions, and customer feedback. Regularly reviewing these factors keeps the pulse on your business and helps you identify potential opportunities for improvement or necessary pivots early. This proactive approach enables you to adapt before challenges escalate.

8. **Stay Resilient in the Face of Change**: Embrace change with resilience. Understand that pivots come with challenges, and it is normal to face uncertainty during transitions. Cultivating resilience allows you to remain focused and motivated, even in the face of setbacks. By reinforcing a positive mindset, you can inspire your team to adapt and thrive amid change.

In conclusion, the pivot mindset is an essential component of entrepreneurship. The ability to recognize when change is necessary and to embrace that change can lead to innovation, growth, and sustained success. Challenges and setbacks are not roadblocks; they are opportunities to evaluate your strategies, gain insights, and adapt accordingly.

By maintaining an open and flexible approach, entrepreneurs can navigate the ever-changing landscape and emerge stronger, more innovative, and more aligned with customer needs. The stories of successful pivots—from Twitter to Netflix to

Instagram—serve as powerful reminders of the potential for transformation that lies within challenges.

As you move forward in your entrepreneurial journey, foster a pivot mindset that embraces change, values learning, and encourages innovation. By doing so, you will not only strengthen your business but also position yourself to lead with agility and confidence in an ever-evolving world.

Reflection

Reflect on a time when you faced significant challenges in your entrepreneurial journey. Did you recognize the need for a pivot? If so, what changes did you make, and how did they impact your business? Write down one potential pivot you think could benefit your current situation or project. Consider the steps you need to take to implement this change effectively. Embrace the opportunity to pivot and harness its power for your growth and success.

Chapter 11

Overcoming Imposter Syndrome

Recognizing self-doubt and affirming your value.

Imposter syndrome is a pervasive feeling of self-doubt, inadequacy, and fear of being exposed as a fraud, despite evidence of one's accomplishments and capabilities. It is an all-too-common experience among entrepreneurs, especially in a landscape filled with uncertainty and competition. In this chapter, we will explore the nature of imposter syndrome, recognize its signs, and provide actionable strategies to overcome these feelings of self-doubt and affirm your value.

Understanding Imposter Syndrome

Imposter syndrome can affect anyone—regardless of their level of success, education, or experience. It manifests as an internal dialogue that questions your abilities and worth. Individuals experiencing imposter syndrome often attribute their achievements to luck or external factors rather than recognizing their skills and hard work.

1. **Common Signs of Imposter Syndrome**:

   o **Self-Doubt**: You constantly question your abilities and feel like you are not qualified for your position or achievements.

   o **Fear of Exposure**: You live in fear of being "found out," believing that others will soon discover you are not as competent as they think.

- o **Discounting Success**: You brush off compliments and accomplishments, attributing them to luck or external circumstances rather than your own efforts.

- o **Perfectionism**: Setting unrealistically high standards and feeling disappointed if you do not achieve them, which then reinforces feelings of inadequacy.

Identifying the Roots of Imposter Syndrome

Understanding the roots of your imposter syndrome can help you address it more effectively. Here are some common contributing factors:

1. **Unrealistic Comparisons**: In the age of social media, it's easy to fall into the trap of comparing your journey to others'. Social media often showcases curated successes, leading you to believe others are constantly thriving while you struggle.

2. **Cultural and Societal Pressures**: Cultural background and societal expectations can influence how we perceive success and achievement. For example, if you were raised in an environment that emphasized perfectionism or high achievement, you may feel an intense pressure to perform flawlessly.

3. **Previous Experiences**: Past experiences of criticism, failure, or challenging feedback can contribute to feelings of self-doubt and inadequacy. Negative experiences create mental roadblocks that linger and impact how you view your current abilities.

Strategies for Overcoming Imposter Syndrome

1. **Acknowledge and Own Your Accomplishments**

Start by acknowledging and celebrating your achievements—no matter how small they may seem. Create a list of your accomplishments, skills, and strengths. Reflect on the hard work and dedication that contributed to these successes. Focus on the tangible evidence of your abilities, and remind yourself that you are deserving of your achievements.

2. **Practice Self-Compassion**

Replace self-criticism with self-compassion. Recognize that everyone experiences self-doubt and that it's a natural part of the journey. Treat yourself with kindness and understanding, just as you would a friend facing similar feelings.

3. **Reframe Negative Self-Talk**

Become aware of the negative thought patterns associated with imposter syndrome. Challenge these thoughts by reframing them into positive affirmations. For instance, instead of thinking, "I'm not qualified to lead this project," try reframing it to, "I have valuable skills to contribute, and I am capable of learning and growing."

4. **Seek Support and Mentorship**

Engaging in open conversations with trusted friends, family members, or mentors can alleviate feelings of isolation. Sharing your experiences with others can provide perspective and reassurance. Mentorship can also help by providing guidance, validation, and encouragement as you navigate your entrepreneurial journey.

5. **Limit Social Comparisons**

Reduce the influence of social media and comparisons that trigger feelings of inadequacy. Curate your feeds to focus on positive, inspiring content and unfollow accounts that contribute to negative self-perception. Instead of comparing yourself to others, focus on your own journey and progress.

6. **Set Realistic Expectations**

Understand that perfection is not attainable. Set realistic and achievable goals for yourself, and allow room for failure and growth. Embrace the idea that making mistakes is part of the learning process, and each setback provides an opportunity for improvement and development.

7. **Keep a "Brag Book"**

Creating a "brag book" or a success journal can provide a tangible way to record your accomplishments, positive feedback, and moments of success. When you experience self-doubt, refer back to this collection to remind yourself of your worth and capabilities.

The Power of Affirmation

Affirmations are simple yet powerful statements that can reshape your beliefs and boost self-confidence. Practice repeating positive affirmations regularly to help combat imposter syndrome:

- "I am knowledgeable and skilled in my field."

- "My contributions are valuable and meaningful."

- "I have earned my success through hard work and dedication."

- "It's okay to ask for help and seek guidance."

- "Challenges are opportunities for growth and learning."

Incorporating these affirmations into your daily routine allows you to replace negative self-talk with empowering thoughts. Over time, these repeated affirmations can significantly shift your mindset and bolster your self-confidence.

Real-Life Examples of Overcoming Imposter Syndrome

Many successful entrepreneurs have experienced imposter syndrome, yet they managed to overcome it through various strategies:

1. **Howard Schultz, CEO of Starbucks**: Schultz has openly discussed his encounters with self-doubt. Despite his success in building Starbucks into a global brand, he admitted to feelings of inadequacy early in his career. Schultz sought mentorship and guidance, ultimately learning to embrace his experiences and recognize his unique contributions to the company. His ability to share his journey has also inspired countless entrepreneurs dealing with similar feelings.

2. **Reshma Saujani, Founder of Girls Who Code**: Saujani experienced imposter syndrome after launching her nonprofit organization. To combat self-doubt, she engaged her support network, sought guidance from mentors, and focused on the mission of empowering young women in tech. By reframing

her narrative, she recognized her value and the impact she could make, ultimately leading to the organization's success.

3. **Maya Angelou, Renowned Author and Poet**: Even after receiving numerous accolades and awards, Angelou experienced imposter syndrome, famously saying, "I have written eleven books, but each time I think, 'Uh-oh, they're going to find out now. I've run a game on everybody, and they're going to find me out.'" Angelou embraced her vulnerabilities and continued to create art that resonated with millions, inspiring others to embrace their own complicated feelings of self-doubt.

As we conclude this chapter on overcoming imposter syndrome, it's important to recognize that self-doubt is a common experience among entrepreneurs and can serve as a signal for growth rather than a hindrance. By acknowledging these feelings and employing the strategies discussed, you can begin to dismantle the barriers that self-doubt creates and affirm your value.

Imposter syndrome may arise from time to time, but it does not define your worth. Combat it with reflection, support, and self-compassion. Embrace your accomplishments, acknowledge your expertise, and recognize that you are deserving of success. By tackling imposter syndrome head-on, you empower yourself to continue your journey in entrepreneurship with confidence and conviction.

Remember, every entrepreneur faces challenges, and being authentic about your experiences only fosters a culture of openness and support within the entrepreneurial community. The more you share your journey and your struggles, the more you'll inspire others to do the same, creating a supportive network that affirms everyone's value.

Reflection

Take a moment to reflect on any feelings of imposter syndrome you've experienced in your own journey. What specific moments triggered these feelings? Write down at least three accomplishments you are proud of or skills you bring to your entrepreneurial endeavors. Finally, set a personal affirmation you will commit to repeating daily— one that resonates with your values and serves as a reminder of your worth. Embrace your journey and celebrate the unique contributions you bring to the world.

Chapter 12

Being Unforgettable

Building a reputation and presence that stands out in the market.

In a crowded marketplace filled with competition and noise, standing out is essential for success as an entrepreneur. The ability to build a reputation and presence that resonates with your audience is what makes you unforgettable. Being unforgettable goes beyond mere visibility; it involves creating a lasting impression that fosters loyalty, engagement, and goodwill. In this chapter, we will explore strategies for building an unforgettable personal and business brand that distinguishes you in the market.

The Importance of Being Unforgettable

1. **Creating Lasting Connections**: An unforgettable brand elicits emotional connections with its audience. When customers feel a bond with your brand, they are more likely to remain loyal, share their experiences with others, and become advocates for your business.

2. **Differentiating from the Competition**: In a saturated market, uniqueness is a competitive advantage. An unforgettable presence helps you carve out a distinct identity that sets you apart from competitors. It positions you as an innovator, leader, or authority within your industry.

3. **Fostering Trust and Credibility**: A strong reputation builds trust. When customers perceive your brand as reliable and valuable, they are more likely to engage with your products or services and recommend you to

others. Trust fosters long-term loyalty and positive word-of-mouth, which is invaluable for business growth.

Building Your Unforgettable Brand

1. Define Your Brand Values and Mission

The foundation of an unforgettable presence begins with a clear understanding of your brand's values and mission. Ask yourself:

- What principles guide my business?

- What unique value do I provide to my customers?

- How do I want my brand to be perceived in the market?

By defining your brand values, you create a cohesive identity that resonates with your audience. Ensuring consistency between your values and your actions fosters authenticity, making your brand more relatable and memorable.

2. Craft a Compelling Brand Story

Storytelling is a powerful tool for making your brand unforgettable. A compelling brand story communicates your journey, vision, and the passions that led you to create your business. Personal stories draw people in, creating emotional connections that resonate on a deeper level.

Consider incorporating elements such as:

- Challenges you faced and overcame,

- Key moments that shaped your brand,

- The reason you are passionate about your work.

Your story should reflect authenticity and invite your audience to feel invested in your journey.

3. **Create a Strong Visual Identity**

Visual elements play a critical role in a memorable brand. Develop a cohesive visual identity that includes a distinct logo, color palette, and typography. Consistent branding creates recognition and reinforces your message across various platforms.

Ensure that your visual identity aligns with your brand story and values, creating an immediate connection to your mission and offerings. Utilize these elements in marketing materials, social media, and your website to create a cohesive presence.

4. **Leverage Social Media and Online Presence**

In today's digital landscape, your online presence can make or break your brand's memorability. Establish a strong social media presence that allows you to engage with your audience regularly. Authentic interaction fosters connection, and sharing valuable content reinforces your reputation as an authority in your industry.

To build an unforgettable online presence:

- Share insights, stories, and tips that resonate with your audience.
- Utilize different formats—videos, graphics, articles—to cater to various preferences.

- Engage with followers by responding to comments, sharing their content, and acknowledging their feedback.

5. **Offer Exceptional Customer Experience**

Your interactions with customers can significantly impact your brand's reputation. Going the extra mile to provide exceptional customer service creates positive experiences that leave a lasting impression.

Consider the following strategies for enhancing customer experience:

- Personalize interactions by remembering names and preferences.

- Follow up after purchases to ensure satisfaction.

- Resolve complaints swiftly and empathetically.

When customers feel valued and appreciated, they are more likely to remember their experience with your brand and share their positive impressions with others.

Developing Unique Differentiators

1. **Identify Your Unique Selling Proposition (USP)**

Your Unique Selling Proposition (USP) is the factor that makes your product or service distinct from competitors. Identify what sets you apart and capitalize on it in your branding. Whether it's superior quality, innovative features, or exceptional customer service, a strong USP strengthens your presence in the market.

2. **Cultivate Expertise and Authority**

Establishing yourself as an authority in your field enhances your brand's reputation. Share your expertise through workshops, webinars, blogs, or podcasts. By positioning yourself as a thought leader, you not only increase your visibility but also build trust with your audience.

Building Authentic Relationships

1. **Network Effectively**

Building relationships with others in your industry can significantly enhance your visibility and reputation. Attend industry events, join professional organizations, and engage in online communities. Networking provides opportunities to collaborate, share knowledge, and gain insights that can elevate your brand.

2. **Seek Collaborations and Partnerships**

Strategic collaborations with other brands or influencers can amplify your presence. Look for partnerships with businesses that share similar values or target audiences to create mutually beneficial relationships. Collaborative ventures can enhance your visibility, introduce you to new audiences, and elevate your brand's reputation through association.

3. **Be Genuine and Authentic**

Authenticity is key to building lasting relationships and an unforgettable brand. Be genuine in your interactions and stay true to your values, even when faced with challenges. People are drawn to authenticity, and your transparency encourages trust and loyalty. When others see you as a real person—not just a brand—they are more likely to connect and remember you.

Staying Relevant Over Time

1. **Continuously Evolve Your Brand**

As markets change and customer preferences shift, it's crucial to stay relevant. Regularly evaluate your branding and offerings to identify areas for improvement. Gather feedback from customers and adapt your strategies based on their needs and insights. Being open to change and willing to evolve will ensure that your brand remains memorable in a rapidly changing environment.

2. **Monitor Trends and Innovations**

Stay informed about trends in your industry and beyond. This awareness allows you to anticipate shifts in consumer behavior and adapt your strategies accordingly. By incorporating current trends and innovations into your offerings, you demonstrate that your brand is progressive and in tune with your audience.

3. **Reinforce Brand Loyalty**

Brand loyalty is cultivated through consistent, positive experiences. Continue to engage with your audience after initial contact. Implement loyalty programs, newsletters, or exclusive events to show appreciation for their support. Building a solid customer base that advocates for your brand ensures that you remain unforgettable long after the first experience.

Being unforgettable is not just about standing out; it's about building a brand that resonates deeply with your audience and fosters long-term relationships. By defining your values, crafting compelling stories, delivering exceptional customer experiences, and continuously evolving, you create a presence that people remember and cherish.

As you embark on your journey to create an unforgettable brand, focus on authenticity, connection, and value. Embrace the uniqueness of your story and share it openly, inviting others to become part of it. The stronger your reputation and presence in the market, the more likely you are to engage and retain loyal customers who advocate for your business.

Your journey as an entrepreneur is a powerful narrative of growth, resilience, and impact. Make it unforgettable—not just for yourself but for everyone who encounters your brand. By doing so, you set the stage for success that transcends transactions and establishes a lasting legacy.

Reflection

Take a moment to reflect on your current brand presence. What makes your brand unique? How do you want others to perceive your business? Write down at least three specific actions you will take in the coming weeks to elevate your brand and ensure it is unforgettable. Whether it's refining your story, enhancing customer interactions, or engaging with your audience more effectively, commit to making your brand stand out in a meaningful way.

Chapter 13
The Art of Idea Generation
Techniques for brainstorming and innovating
business ideas.

In the fast-paced world of entrepreneurship, the ability to generate innovative ideas is critical to staying ahead of the competition and succeeding in your endeavors. Idea generation is not just a single moment of inspiration; it's an ongoing process that requires creativity, collaboration, and strategic thinking. In this chapter, we will explore various techniques for brainstorming and generating business ideas, as well as how to cultivate an environment that fosters continuous innovation.

Understanding the Importance of Idea Generation

1. **Fueling Innovation**: New ideas drive innovation, enabling businesses to adapt and evolve in response to changing market dynamics. Cultivating a habit of idea generation keeps your business fresh and competitive.

2. **Identifying Opportunities**: Effective idea generation helps entrepreneurs uncover gaps in the market and identify unmet consumer needs. When you prioritize idea generation, you increase your chances of discovering unique value propositions that resonate with your audience.

3. **Encouraging Problem-Solving**: Generating ideas is an essential part of problem-solving. When

presented with challenges, brainstorming potential solutions encourages creative thinking and collaboration within your team, leading to effective outcomes.

Techniques for Idea Generation

1. Brainstorming Sessions

One of the most common techniques for idea generation is brainstorming, which involves gathering a group of people to discuss ideas without judgment. The goal is to generate a large volume of ideas and encourage free-flowing thought.

Tips for Effective Brainstorming:

- **Set a Clear Focus**: Clearly define the topic or challenge you want to address. Frame the problem to ensure all participants understand the goal.

- **Create a Safe Space**: Encourage an open, non-judgmental environment where all ideas are welcome. Promote an atmosphere that fosters creativity.

- **Use Prompts**: Start with prompts or questions to stimulate discussion. For example, "What if we could eliminate one step in our customer process?" helps to open up creative thinking.

- **Time Box Sessions**: Designate a specific timeframe for brainstorming (e.g., 20-30 minutes) to keep the session focused and energetic.

2. Mind Mapping

Mind mapping is a visual technique that helps organize thoughts and ideas around a central concept. This technique allows you to see connections and generate additional ideas from the primary idea.

How to Mind Map:

- Start with a central idea written in the middle of a page.

- Branch out with related ideas, concepts, or themes.

- Use colors, images, and keywords to enhance the visual appeal and make it easier to identify connections.

Mind mapping not only stimulates creative thinking but also helps clarify the relationships between different ideas.

3. SCAMPER Technique

The SCAMPER technique is a creative problem-solving method that encourages innovation by prompting you to think about existing products or services in new ways. SCAMPER is an acronym for:

- **S**ubstitute: What can be substituted or replaced in your product or process?

- **C**ombine: What ideas can be combined to create something new?

- **A**dapt: How can you adapt or adjust your current offerings?

- **M**odify: Can you modify aspects of your product or service to improve it?

- **P**ut to another use: How can your product or service be used differently?

- **E**liminate: What can be eliminated to improve efficiency or effectiveness?

- **R**everse: What can be reversed or rearranged to create new ideas?

This structured approach encourages you to critically analyze and reimagine ideas, leading to innovative developments.

4. **Role-Playing and Scenario Creation**

Role-playing involves stepping into the shoes of different stakeholders (customers, employees, competitors) to explore ideas and perspectives. This technique helps uncover insights and generates ideas that you may not have considered otherwise.

How to Implement Role-Playing:

- Define the scenario or problem you want to address.

- Assign roles to team members—each representing a stakeholder perspective.

- Conduct the role-play, allowing participants to engage as if they are living the situation.

This immersive approach can illuminate customer needs, pain points, and opportunities for innovation.

5. **Change the Environment**

Sometimes a change of scenery can spark new ideas. Shifting your environment can stimulate creativity and encourage fresh thinking.

Tips for Changing the Environment:

- **Work Outdoors**: Take brainstorming sessions outside to a park or a café.

- **Visit Different Spaces**: Explore different workspaces (co-working environments, art studios) to inspire creativity.

- **Incorporate Art and Design**: Infuse your space with artwork or creative materials that encourage imaginative thinking.

Changing your routine or environment can unlock unexpected insights and ideas.

Cultivating a Culture of Innovation

1. Encourage Diverse Thinking

Diversity fosters innovative thinking. Encourage team members from various backgrounds and disciplines to contribute their unique perspectives during brainstorming sessions. This diversity can lead to richer discussions and more creative solutions.

2. Provide Resources and Time for Creativity

It's essential to prioritize time and resources for creative thinking. Allocate specific hours each week for brainstorming and idea generation activities. Provide access to materials that inspire creativity, such as books, articles, and tools for collaboration. Consider introducing creative workshops, training sessions, or retreats that focus solely on innovation and idea generation.

3. Celebrate Ideas and Innovations

Create an environment where innovation is celebrated. Recognize and reward employees who contribute valuable ideas, whether they lead to successful projects or serve as learning opportunities. Celebrating both successful and failed ideas creates a culture of experimentation, where team members feel encouraged to take risks and share their thoughts without fear of judgment.

4. Implement an Idea Management System

An idea management system allows you to collect, organize, and assess ideas over time. This can be a digital platform or a dedicated physical space where team members can submit their ideas. Regularly review and discuss submissions, allowing individuals to feel involved in the innovation process. This system not only encourages continuous idea generation but also helps ensure that valuable ideas do not get lost in the shuffle.

As we conclude this chapter on the art of idea generation, it's crucial to understand that generating ideas is not a one-time event but a lifelong practice. The ability to brainstorm, innovate, and adapt continuously is vital for success in entrepreneurship.

By employing the techniques discussed—brainstorming sessions, mind mapping, SCAMPER, role-playing, and environmental changes—you can cultivate a vibrant pipeline of ideas that will drive your business forward. Building a culture of innovation requires commitment and openness to experimentation. It invites collaboration and enables every team member to contribute to the collective vision.

Remember, great ideas can lead to revolutionary changes and significant advancements for your business. Every successful entrepreneur knows that the journey of innovation is fueled by creativity and the willingness to explore the unknown. Embrace the art of idea generation, and let your curiosity guide you toward new pathways of success.

Reflection

Take a moment to reflect on your current idea generation practices. What techniques do you typically use, and how effective are they? Write down at least three new methods you'd like to experiment with to enhance your brainstorming processes. Choose a specific challenge or area of your business that you would like to address using these new techniques. Commit to implementing these strategies in the coming weeks to foster creativity and innovation in your entrepreneurial journey.

Chapter 14

Seeing Potential Where Others Don't

Identifying opportunities in gaps and unmet needs in the market.

In the world of entrepreneurship, the ability to identify opportunities in gaps and unmet needs within the market sets successful entrepreneurs apart from the rest. While many may see challenges or saturation, true visionaries possess the insight to recognize potential where others overlook it. This chapter will explore the mindset required to see potential in every situation, strategies to identify market gaps, and how to leverage those insights to create innovative opportunities.

The Mindset of a Visionary

1. **Curiosity-Driven Approach**: Visionary entrepreneurs maintain a sense of curiosity that compels them to explore and understand the world around them. This intellectual curiosity allows them to question the status quo, ask "why," and dig deeper to uncover underlying issues and opportunities. Embrace a mindset that constantly seeks to learn and discover, as this curiosity will lead you to insights that others may miss.

2. **Embracing a Growth Mindset**: A growth mindset—the belief that skills and intelligence can be developed—empowers entrepreneurs to view

obstacles as opportunities for growth. This mentality fosters resilience and adaptability, allowing you to remain open to new ideas and alternative paths when faced with challenges.

3. **Positive Framing**: Individuals who see potential often reframe negative experiences or challenges as opportunities. This positive framing encourages creative thinking and innovation. Instead of viewing market competition as a threat, see it as a chance to differentiate your offering or improve upon existing solutions.

Strategies for Identifying Opportunities

1. Conduct Market Research

Understanding your industry and target market is foundational in identifying opportunities. Conduct thorough market research to analyze trends, customer preferences, and competitor offerings. Use surveys, interviews, and focus groups to gather direct insights from your target audience. Pay attention to feedback to understand their pain points and desires that are not currently being addressed.

2. Analyze Trends and Forecasts

Trends can provide valuable insights into emerging needs and gaps in the market. Keep a close eye on industry reports, consumer behavior studies, and relevant news articles. Look for patterns that indicate changing preferences or behaviors. For instance, the rise of eco-conscious consumers may signal an opportunity for sustainable products or services. Utilize trend analysis as a tool for forecasting potential opportunities on the horizon.

3. **Identify Pain Points**

Directly addressing customer pain points is perhaps one of the most potent ways to uncover opportunities. Engage with your audience to understand the challenges they face. Social media platforms, online forums, and customer reviews can all provide critical insights into unmet needs. Once you identify recurring pain points, consider how your business can address these issues in innovative ways.

4. **Embrace The "Jobs to Be Done" Framework**

The Jobs to Be Done (JTBD) framework focuses on understanding the underlying goals or tasks that customers are trying to accomplish. Instead of merely segmenting customers by demographic traits, consider what "job" they are hiring a product or service to do. By identifying the functional, social, and emotional jobs customers seek to fill, you can uncover new opportunities to create value and innovate.

5. **Look Beyond Your Industry**

Inspiration for new ideas often comes from unexpected sources. Examine other industries to see how they address similar challenges or market needs. By cross-pollinating ideas, you can bring fresh perspectives to your own business. For example, in the food industry, concepts like meal kits and subscription services emerged from observing successful models in the e-commerce industry.

Leveraging Insights to Create Opportunities

1. **Brainstorm Innovative Solutions**

Once you've identified gaps and needs, gather your team for a brainstorming session focused on generating innovative solutions that address those opportunities. Use techniques such as mind mapping or the SCAMPER method to explore a variety of ideas and possibilities. Encourage creativity and allow the discussion to flow freely without judgment.

2. Prototype and Test Ideas

Before committing significant resources, develop prototypes or pilot programs to test your ideas. This iterative approach enables you to gather feedback, assess viability, and make adjustments as needed. Testing ideas in real-market conditions provides invaluable insights into customer reactions and challenges.

3. Stay Agile and Adaptable

In a rapidly changing market, the ability to pivot and adapt based on new insights is crucial. Be prepared to modify your approach as you gather more information. An agile mindset allows you to continuously refine your offerings and seize emerging opportunities.

4. Build Relationships with Customers

Developing strong relationships with customers fosters loyalty and encourages ongoing feedback. By creating an open dialogue, you can gain deeper insights into their evolving needs. This connection allows you to adapt your products and services over time, ensuring that you continue to address gaps and exceed expectations.

5. Create a Culture of Innovation

Encourage a culture of innovation within your organization, where team members feel empowered to identify opportunities and share their insights. Recognize contributions and celebrate successes, while also embracing lessons learned from failed attempts. When everyone is encouraged to contribute, you cultivate an environment ripe for discovering unmet needs and generating creative solutions.

The Power of Persistence

Identifying opportunities in gaps and unmet needs often requires persistence and patience. The entrepreneurial journey is rarely linear, and obstacles will inevitably arise. It's vital to stay committed to your vision and remain tenacious in pursuing your goals, even when initial efforts do not yield the desired results.

1. **Stay Committed to Learning**: Keep the mindset that every setback is an opportunity to learn and grow. Use challenges as stepping stones to refine your approach and come back stronger. Embracing your failures as part of the journey ensures that you remain resilient and open to future opportunities.

2. **Engage in Continuous Improvement**: Regularly review your progress and the effectiveness of your strategies in identifying opportunities. Solicit feedback from customers, team members, and other stakeholders. Use these insights to make necessary adjustments and remain aligned with emerging needs in the market.

3. **Network and Collaborate**: Build relationships with other entrepreneurs, industry experts, and mentors. Networking provides access to diverse perspectives and insights that can help you identify opportunities that may be outside of your immediate focus. Collaborating with others can also lead to innovative solutions for addressing gaps in the market.

As we conclude this chapter on seeing potential where others don't, it's clear that identifying opportunities in gaps and unmet needs is not just a skill, but a mindset. By fostering curiosity, maintaining a growth-oriented perspective, and actively seeking insights through research and engagement, you position yourself to recognize hidden opportunities that many overlook.

Remember that creativity and innovation often stem from the willingness to ask questions and explore challenges rather than avoid them. Cultivating the ability to see potential requires ongoing effort and a commitment to continuous learning. Embrace the art of idea generation as an integral part of your entrepreneurial journey, allowing it to fuel your business's growth and success.

By adopting this proactive approach, you will not only differentiate yourself in the marketplace but also empower yourself to create more meaningful solutions that resonate with your audience and contribute to your success.

Reflection

Reflect on your current approach to identifying opportunities. What steps can you take to enhance your ability to see potential in gaps and unmet needs? Write down at least three specific techniques or practices you will implement in the next few weeks to develop your skills in opportunity recognition. Whether it's conducting market research, engaging with customers, or expanding your network, commit to ongoing growth and innovation in your entrepreneurial journey.

Chapter 15
Clarity in Chaos

Finding clarity and decision-making in fast-paced environments.

In the realm of entrepreneurship, chaos is a constant companion. The fast-paced nature of the business landscape, characterized by shifting market trends, fluctuating consumer preferences, and unexpected challenges, can quickly lead to confusion and overwhelm. However, the most successful entrepreneurs are those who find clarity amid the chaos. This chapter will explore strategies for achieving clarity in turbulent times, enhancing decision-making, and maintaining focus on your goals.

Understanding the Need for Clarity

1. **Navigating Complexity**: In chaotic environments, decision-making can become complicated due to the numerous variables at play. Clarity helps entrepreneurs sift through complexity, enabling them to identify key priorities and maintain a strategic focus.

2. **Reducing Stress and Anxiety**: The uncertainty of fast-paced environments can lead to heightened stress levels. Clarity fosters confidence in your decisions by empowering you to analyze situations

effectively and trust your instincts, ultimately reducing anxiety.

3. **Driving Effective Action**: Without clarity, it becomes easy to become reactive instead of proactive. A clear understanding of your objectives allows you to take decisive actions that align with your long-term vision, driving results.

Strategies for Achieving Clarity in Chaos

1. Define Your Core Values and Mission

Establishing clear core values and a mission statement serves as a guiding star amid the chaos. These values act as a compass, directing your decision-making and ensuring that your actions align with your overall purpose. Regularly revisit your mission and values to maintain focus.

2. Set Clear Goals

Break down your long-term vision into specific, actionable goals. Use the SMART (Specific, Measurable, Achievable, Relevant, Time-bound) criteria to define your objectives. Clear goals provide focus and help you prioritize your efforts, allowing you to navigate through distractions more effectively.

3. Prioritize and Simplify

When faced with multiple tasks and decisions, prioritize your actions based on urgency and impact. Create a simple matrix to assess tasks and determine which activities align most closely with your goals. Learning to simplify the complex allows you to focus on what truly matters.

4. Establish a Routine

Creating a daily or weekly routine can provide you with a sense of structure and control amid chaos. Designate specific times for critical tasks, project reviews, and reflection. Routines help reinforce good habits, reduce decision fatigue, and create a stable environment conducive to clarity.

5. Practice Mindfulness and Reflection

Mindfulness practices—such as meditation, deep breathing, or journaling—enhance self-awareness and promote mental clarity. Setting aside time for reflection allows you to evaluate your decisions, assess your progress, and adapt your strategies as needed. This practice keeps you grounded and focused amidst the hustle of daily operations.

6. Gather Reliable Data and Insights

In chaotic environments, information can flow in unpredictably, making it essential to have reliable data at your disposal. Regularly monitor key performance indicators (KPIs) and gather insights from market research, customer feedback, and industry reports. Data-driven decision-making empowers you to navigate uncertainties with confidence.

Decision-Making in a Chaotic Environment

1. Leverage the 70% Rule

One effective strategy for decision-making in chaos is the "70% Rule." This principle suggests that you shouldn't wait for 100% certainty before making decisions. Instead, aim for around 70% confidence in your assessment. This approach encourages timely decisions while acknowledging that some uncertainty will always exist. Acting with urgency can prevent analysis paralysis and keep your momentum moving forward.

2. Engage Your Team

Tap into the collective knowledge and perspectives of your team when making decisions. Encourage open discussions and solicit input from different departments or stakeholders. Collaborative decision-making fosters diversity of thought, leading to more informed and well-rounded choices.

3. Develop Contingency Plans

Planning for potential setbacks helps reduce stress and enhances your ability to adapt when the unexpected occurs. Create contingency plans for key areas of your business, outlining what actions you would take in response to various scenarios. This proactive approach allows you to navigate challenges more effectively when they arise.

4. Embrace Iterative Decision-Making

In a rapidly changing environment, it's essential to embrace iterative decision-making. Instead of seeking complete certainty before moving forward, make decisions based on the best available information, then monitor results and be prepared to adjust as needed. This approach allows you to test hypotheses, learn from outcomes, and refine your strategies continuously.

Maintaining Focus and Direction

1. Stay Aligned with Your Vision

Amidst distractions and chaos, regularly revisit your overarching vision. Use visual reminders—such as vision boards or mission statements—to keep your goals in the forefront of your mind. Staying aligned with your vision reaffirms your purpose and motivates you to navigate uncertainties with clarity and conviction.

2. Limit Distractions

Identify and minimize distractions that disrupt your focus. This could include setting boundaries around meetings, managing notifications, or allocating specific times for checking emails and messages. Creating a focused work environment fosters clarity and enhances your productivity, allowing you to concentrate on the tasks that contribute to your goals.

3. **Regularly Assess and Adapt**

In a chaotic environment, it's crucial to continuously assess your performance and strategies. Implement regular checkpoints—whether weekly or monthly—to evaluate your progress toward goals, review your decision-making processes, and determine if any adjustments are needed. This proactive assessment keeps you flexible and allows you to pivot if necessary while maintaining clarity in your objectives.

4. **Utilize Tools and Technology**

Leverage technology to streamline operations and enhance clarity. Utilize project management tools, scheduling software, and communication platforms to organize tasks, set priorities, and facilitate collaboration. These tools help provide a clear overview of responsibilities and deadlines, reducing confusion in a fast-paced environment.

As we conclude this chapter on finding clarity in chaos, remember that uncertainty is an inherent aspect of entrepreneurship. The ability to navigate this chaos and make informed decisions is what sets successful entrepreneurs apart. By fostering a mindset focused on clarity and employing the strategies discussed, you empower yourself to thrive in dynamic environments.

Clarity leads to confidence in decision-making and allows you to remain centered amidst change. Remember to ground yourself in your core values, keep your goals in sight, and involve your team in the decision-making process. By doing so, you cultivate an environment that not only embraces change but also thrives on it.

As you face the inevitable chaos of the entrepreneurial landscape, approach challenges with a steady mind and a clear vision. Embrace the opportunities for growth that chaos presents, and let clarity be your guiding light on the path toward success.

Reflection

Take a moment to reflect on the current state of your entrepreneurial journey. What areas of chaos do you experience frequently? Write down three specific strategies from this chapter that you will implement to enhance clarity in your decision-making and leadership. Whether it's creating a structured routine, engaging your team, or utilizing data-driven insights, commit to taking action to embrace clarity in the midst of chaos.

Chapter 16

The Gratitude Advantage

Using gratitude to open doors and foster relationships.

In the fast-paced and often stressful world of entrepreneurship, it's easy to overlook the simple yet profound power of gratitude. Cultivating a mindset of gratitude not only enhances personal well-being but also serves as a powerful tool for entrepreneurs to build relationships, foster loyalty, and open doors to new opportunities. In this chapter, we will explore the concept of gratitude, its benefits in the entrepreneurial landscape, and practical strategies for incorporating gratitude into your daily life and business practices.

Understanding the Power of Gratitude

1. **Fostering Positive Mindsets**: Gratitude is more than just saying "thank you"; it is a mindset that allows individuals to appreciate what they have rather than focusing on what they lack. This positive outlook can lead to greater satisfaction, resilience, and happiness, which are essential traits for entrepreneurs facing frequent challenges and uncertainties.

2. **Enhancing Emotional Intelligence**: Practicing gratitude boosts emotional intelligence by helping individuals recognize and appreciate the contributions of others. This heightened awareness allows for better interpersonal relationships,

improved communication, and a greater ability to empathize with others.

3. **Reducing Stress and Anxiety**: Gratitude helps mitigate feelings of stress and anxiety by shifting focus from negative aspects of life to positive experiences and relationships. This shift can improve overall well-being, leading to greater focus and productivity in business endeavors.

The Benefits of Gratitude in Entrepreneurship

1. **Building Strong Relationships**: One of the most significant advantages of expressing gratitude is its ability to foster strong relationships with team members, clients, mentors, and partners. When people feel appreciated and valued, trust grows, laying the foundation for collaboration and loyalty.

2. **Enhancing Networking Opportunities**: Gratitude can expand your network by encouraging authentic connections with others. When you express genuine appreciation for someone's support or guidance, it creates a lasting impression. This memory can lead to referrals, new partnerships, and increased collaboration.

3. **Motivating and Engaging Employees**: In a workplace culture grounded in gratitude, employees feel more valued and engaged. When leaders recognize their team members' efforts and contributions, it boosts morale and productivity. This culture of appreciation creates a motivated workforce that is more likely to go above and beyond.

4. **Creating a Positive Reputation**: An entrepreneur who practices gratitude and appreciation not only builds strong relationships but also cultivates a positive reputation within their industry and community. This reputation can open doors to new opportunities, partnerships, and customer loyalty.

Strategies for Practicing Gratitude

1. Establish a Gratitude Ritual

Incorporate gratitude into your daily routine by establishing a gratitude ritual. This could be as simple as taking a few moments each morning to reflect on things for which you are grateful. You might write them in a journal, share them with a colleague, or voice them in a personal meditation. This practice helps set a positive tone for your day and encourages a grateful mindset.

2. Express Appreciation Regularly

Make it a point to express appreciation to those around you—both in your personal and professional life. This can be done through verbal acknowledgments, handwritten notes, or simple messages. Recognizing the efforts of your team members, colleagues, and partners fosters a culture of gratitude and strengthens relationships.

3. Celebrate Wins, Big and Small

Take time to celebrate accomplishments, both big and small. Acknowledging achievements reinforces a sense of gratitude within your team or business. Host team celebrations or simple shout-outs to recognize milestones, successful projects, or individual contributions. This recognition motivates continued efforts and cultivates a positive atmosphere.

4. Utilize Social Media for Gratitude

Leverage social media platforms to express gratitude publicly. Share posts that recognize the contributions of team members, mentors, or collaborators. Highlighting others reinforces your appreciation and can inspire others to practice gratitude in their own networks.

5. Create a Gratitude Board

Consider creating a gratitude board where team members can share what they are thankful for in a visible and engaging way. This could be a physical board in the office or a digital version shared within your organization. This collaborative effort not only fosters connection but also encourages a positive workplace culture.

6. Mentorship and Giving Back

Gratitude can also manifest in the form of mentorship and giving back. Share your knowledge, skills, and experiences with others looking to grow in your industry. Actively mentoring someone can create a powerful ripple effect of gratitude, fostering relationships that contribute to both personal and professional growth.

The Long-Term Impact of Gratitude

1. **Resilience and Adaptability**: A grateful mindset cultivates resilience, allowing entrepreneurs to navigate challenges with a positive outlook. Grateful individuals are more likely to embrace setbacks as opportunities for growth, which fuels adaptability in the face of adversity.

2. **Strengthened Communities**: Practicing gratitude extends beyond individual relationships; it contributes to the overall health of communities and industries. When gratitude becomes a shared value, it fosters a culture of support and encouragement, strengthening the bonds within groups and enhancing collaboration.

3. **Enhanced Well-Being**: Over the long term, gratitude contributes to improved mental health and emotional well-being. Entrepreneurs who regularly practice gratitude report lower levels of stress, anxiety, and depression. This enhanced well-being not only benefits the individual but also creates a ripple effect within their organization, promoting a positive work environment.

4. **Increased Creativity and Innovation**: Grateful individuals often experience greater levels of creativity and innovation. The positive mindset cultivated through gratitude opens the mind to new ideas and possibilities, leading to enhanced problem-solving skills and a more innovative approach to business challenges.

As we wrap up this chapter on the gratitude advantage, it's clear that cultivating a practice of gratitude can significantly impact your personal well-being and professional relationships. Gratitude is not just a fleeting expression; it is a powerful mindset that has the potential to transform how you engage with others and navigate the challenges of entrepreneurship.

By consciously embracing gratitude in your daily life and business practices, you can build stronger relationships, foster loyalty, and create a positive reputation. The benefits of gratitude extend far beyond personal satisfaction, contributing to a thriving community of collaboration and innovation.

As you move forward in your entrepreneurial journey, make it a priority to practice gratitude intentionally. Recognize the contributions of those around you, celebrate achievements, and cultivate a culture of appreciation within your business. The more you practice gratitude, the more you will unlock the doors to new opportunities and enrich your professional relationships.

Reflection

Take a moment to reflect on your current practice of gratitude. How often do you express appreciation to those around you? Write down three people you are grateful for in your personal or professional life, along with specific reasons for your gratitude. Additionally, identify one actionable step you will take in the coming week to incorporate gratitude into your daily routine—whether it's a simple thank-you note, a social media shout-out, or a verbal acknowledgment. Commit to embracing the gratitude advantage and witness its positive impact on your entrepreneurial journey.

Chapter 17

Wellness in Wealth

Balancing physical and mental health while pursuing success.

In the pursuit of success and financial prosperity, many entrepreneurs overlook one critical component: their health. The stereotype of the relentless entrepreneur who thrives on long hours without rest is not only unsustainable but can also be detrimental to both personal well-being and business success. Balancing physical and mental health while striving for wealth is essential for sustaining high performance, creativity, and longevity in your career. This chapter will explore the importance of wellness in wealth, practical strategies for achieving balance, and how prioritizing health can enhance both personal and professional outcomes.

The Importance of Wellness

1. **Sustainability**: True success is not just measured by financial achievements but also by the ability to sustain those achievements over time. Physical and mental wellness are foundational to maintaining the energy and focus needed to work effectively and make sound decisions.

2. **Enhanced Performance**: Prioritizing health leads to improved cognitive function, creativity, and productivity. Entrepreneurs who invest in their well-being are better equipped to handle stress, solve

problems, and innovate—essential traits for navigating the challenges of entrepreneurship.

3. **Increased Resilience**: Mental and physical wellness contribute to emotional resilience. When entrepreneurs prioritize their health, they develop the tools needed to cope with stress, bounce back from setbacks, and stay focused on their long-term goals.

4. **Improved Relationships**: A healthy entrepreneur is often a happier and more engaged individual. Prioritizing wellness allows you to foster deeper connections with your team, clients, and network. Healthy relationships are essential for building support systems that contribute to enduring success.

Strategies for Achieving Wellness in Wealth

1. **Prioritize Physical Well-Being**

   o **Regular Exercise**: Incorporating physical activity into your routine has numerous benefits for both body and mind. Aim for at least 30 minutes of moderate exercise most days of the week. This could include activities such as walking, jogging, cycling, or yoga. Regular exercise boosts energy levels, improves mood, and enhances overall well-being.

   o **Balanced Nutrition**: Fueling your body with nutritious foods is vital for maintaining energy and focus. Strive for a balanced diet that includes a variety of fruits, vegetables, lean proteins, and whole grains. Avoid excessive caffeine, sugar, and highly processed foods—

opt for wholesome alternatives that nourish your body.

- o **Adequate Sleep**: Sleep is a cornerstone of physical and mental health. Aim for 7-9 hours of quality sleep each night, prioritizing rest to allow your body and mind to rejuvenate. Establish a calming bedtime routine, limit screen time before bed, and create a conducive sleep environment.

2. **Nurture Mental Wellness**

- o **Mindfulness and Meditation**: Practicing mindfulness and meditation can significantly enhance mental clarity and reduce anxiety. Set aside time each day to engage in mindfulness activities, whether through meditation, deep breathing exercises, or journaling. These practices promote self-awareness and help you maintain focus amidst chaos.

- o **Stress Management**: Identify the sources of stress in your life and develop effective coping strategies. Techniques may include time management, prioritization, and engaging in leisure activities that bring joy. Don't hesitate to seek professional support or counseling when facing particularly challenging times.

- o **Set Boundaries**: Establish clear boundaries between work and personal life. Protect your time and make intentional choices about when to unplug from work. Communicate these boundaries to your team and stick to them, allowing yourself to recharge and rejuvenate outside of work hours.

3. **Foster Positive Relationships**

   o **Surround Yourself with Supportive People**: Build a network of supportive individuals who uplift and inspire you. Cultivating relationships with mentors, peers, and friends who value wellness creates an encouraging environment that fosters personal and professional growth.

   o **Regular Check-Ins**: Make it a habit to check in with yourself and your loved ones about well-being. Discuss stressors, achievements, and feelings. This open communication strengthens relationships and helps identify when others may need support.

4. **Integrate Wellness into Your Business Culture**

   o **Promote Wellness Initiatives**: If you lead a team, prioritize wellness initiatives within your organization. Encourage breaks, provide access to wellness resources, and create opportunities for physical activity, such as walking meetings or group fitness classes. A culture that values wellness fosters a happier and more productive team.

   o **Flexible Work Arrangements**: Consider implementing flexible work arrangements that allow team members to prioritize their own health. Flexibility in hours, remote work options, and wellness days can contribute significantly to employee motivation and satisfaction.

The Long-Term Benefits of Prioritizing Wellness

1. **Sustained Success**: Prioritizing wellness leads to a more sustainable approach to enterprise growth. Healthy entrepreneurs are better equipped to manage the inevitable ups and downs of their journey, maintain focus on their objectives, and adapt to change over time.

2. **Increased Creativity and Innovation**: A healthy body and mind are fertile ground for creativity. By nurturing your wellness, you open yourself up to new ideas and perspectives that can fuel innovation. When you feel physically and mentally well, you are more alert, focused, and engaged, which enhances your problem-solving capabilities and ability to think creatively.

3. **Better Decision-Making**: Well-being contributes to improved cognitive function, which directly influences decision-making processes. When you prioritize your health, you reduce stress and mental fog, enabling you to make clearer, more rational decisions based on sound judgment rather than emotional responses.

4. **Enhanced Reputation**: Entrepreneurs who prioritize their wellness and the wellness of their teams often earn a reputation as compassionate leaders. This reputation enhances trust, loyalty, and respect from employees, clients, and industry peers. Being known as a leader who values health and well-being can help attract top talent and loyal clients.

5. **Positive Impact on Communities**: When you embody wellness in your business practices, you set an example for others in your community. By promoting a culture of health and well-being, you can inspire fellow

entrepreneurs and organizations to adopt similar values. This ripple effect can contribute to healthier business ecosystems and communities overall.

As we conclude this chapter on wellness in wealth, it's clear that achieving success as an entrepreneur is not solely about financial growth or market expansion. Prioritizing physical and mental health is essential for sustaining high performance and achieving lasting success.

Remember that wellness is an ongoing journey, one that requires conscious effort, regular assessment, and a willingness to adapt. By incorporating healthy practices into your daily routine and fostering a culture of well-being within your organization, you empower yourself and others to thrive both personally and professionally.

As you move forward in your entrepreneurial journey, embrace the idea that true wealth encompasses not just financial success but overall well-being. Prioritize your health, nurture positive relationships, and cultivate a balanced approach to your work and life. By doing so, you will create a sustainable foundation for ongoing success and fulfillment.

Reflection
Take some time to reflect on your current approach to wellness. Are there areas in which you could improve to balance your health with your entrepreneurial ambitions? Write down three specific actions you can take to enhance your physical and mental well-being in the coming weeks. Consider incorporating healthy habits, setting boundaries, or engaging in activities that bring you joy. Commit to making wellness a priority as you continue your entrepreneurial journey.

Chapter 18

Building Resilience

Strategies for bouncing back from setbacks.

In entrepreneurship, setbacks and challenges are inevitable. Whether it is a failed product launch, an unexpected market shift, or financial difficulties, every entrepreneur will face obstacles on their journey. However, what distinguishes successful entrepreneurs is their resilience—the ability to bounce back and thrive in the face of adversity. In this chapter, we will explore the importance of resilience, the characteristics of resilient individuals, and effective strategies for building and reinforcing your resilience as an entrepreneur.

Understanding Resilience

1. **Definition of Resilience**: Resilience is the capacity to recover quickly from difficulties and adapt to change. It involves not just surviving adversity, but also growing stronger and more capable through the experience. Resilience is an essential attribute for navigating the unpredictable nature of entrepreneurship and maintaining motivation and focus during challenging times.

2. **The Importance of Resilience**: Building resilience is crucial for several reasons:

   o **Sustained Performance**: Resilience allows you to maintain a high level of performance even in the face of challenges. It helps you stay focused on your goals and maintain productivity during tough times.

- ○ **Adaptability**: Resilient entrepreneurs are often more adaptable, willing to pivot and explore alternative paths when faced with hurdles. This flexibility enhances their ability to seize new opportunities.

- ○ **Emotional Well-Being**: Developing resilience can promote better mental health by reducing stress and anxiety. Resilient individuals tend to have stronger coping mechanisms, leading to enhanced emotional stability.

Characteristics of Resilient Entrepreneurs

1. **Positive Mindset**: Resilient entrepreneurs cultivate a positive outlook, viewing challenges as opportunities for growth rather than insurmountable obstacles.

2. **Self-Awareness**: They possess a high degree of self-awareness, recognizing their strengths, weaknesses, and emotional triggers. This understanding allows them to make informed decisions during difficult times.

3. **Strong Problem-Solving Skills**: Resilient individuals are adept at analyzing problems and generating creative solutions. They approach challenges with a mindset of curiosity and resourcefulness.

4. **Supportive Networks**: Resilient entrepreneurs value relationships and actively build supportive networks. They seek help and advice from mentors,

peers, and team members, fostering collaboration and connection.

5. **Commitment to Learning**: Resilient individuals view setbacks as learning opportunities. They embrace a growth mindset and are committed to continuous improvement, viewing failure as a stepping stone to success.

Strategies for Building Resilience

1. Cultivate a Growth Mindset

Adopting a growth mindset is fundamental to building resilience. This mindset involves believing that abilities and intelligence can be developed through dedication and hard work. You can cultivate a growth mindset by:

- Embracing challenges as opportunities to learn and grow.

- Persisting in the face of setbacks and viewing failure as a natural part of the learning process.

- Seeking feedback and using it to improve your skills and strategies.

2. Develop Strong Coping Skills

Establishing effective coping mechanisms is essential for managing stress and maintaining resilience. Some strategies to enhance your coping skills include:

- **Mindfulness and Meditation**: Incorporate mindfulness practices to stay grounded and reduce stress. Techniques such as deep breathing, meditation, or yoga can help you regain focus and calmness during tough times.

- **Physical Activity**: Engage in regular physical exercise to boost your mood, reduce anxiety, and increase overall well-being. Exercise releases endorphins, which are natural stress relievers.

- **Journaling**: Maintaining a journal to document your thoughts, feelings, and experiences can help you process emotions and gain perspective on challenges. Writing can also highlight achievements and remind you of your capacity to overcome obstacles.

3. **Build a Support Network**

Surrounding yourself with a supportive network is crucial for resilience. Seek out relationships with mentors, peers, family, and friends who uplift and encourage you. To build a strong support network:

- **Engage in Networking**: Attend industry events, workshops, and meetups to connect with fellow entrepreneurs and like-minded individuals.

- **Seek Mentorship**: Identify mentors who can provide guidance, wisdom, and encouragement. Their experiences can offer valuable insights during challenging times.

- **Foster Meaningful Relationships**: Establish authentic connections with others, creating an environment of trust where you can share experiences, seek advice, and provide support.

4. **Learn from Setbacks**

When facing a setback, take time to analyze what went wrong and what lessons can be gleaned from the experience. Use the following strategies to transform setbacks into learning opportunities:

- Conduct a post-mortem analysis of the situation. What factors contributed to the setback? Were there warning signs or indicators you missed?

- Identify actionable insights that can be applied moving forward, and create an action plan that leverages these learnings to enhance future decision-making.

- Frame setbacks as "growing pains" and recognize that each challenge contributes to your growth as an entrepreneur.

5. **Establish Clear Goals and Plans**

Having clear goals and plans provides direction and purpose, allowing you to remain focused on your vision even amid challenges. Here are ways to establish clear goals and action plans:

- **Set SMART Goals**: Establish Specific, Measurable, Achievable, Relevant, and Time-bound goals. This clarity not only helps you track your progress but also enables you to break down larger objectives into manageable tasks. When faced with setbacks, having clear goals will help you remember your purpose and stay motivated.
- **Develop Action Plans**: For each goal, create a detailed action plan that outlines the specific steps you need to take, resources required, and timelines for completion. This structure provides a roadmap for overcoming obstacles and staying on course.

- **Regularly Review and Adjust**: Periodically review your goals and plans to assess progress and make necessary adjustments. This ongoing evaluation allows you to stay adaptive and respond effectively to changing circumstances.

6. **Embrace Optimism**

Maintaining a positive outlook can significantly influence your resilience. Optimism is a powerful motivator that encourages you to see beyond immediate challenges and envision a brighter future. To cultivate optimism:

- **Focus on Solutions**: During times of adversity, concentrate on finding solutions instead of dwelling on problems. Train yourself to ask, "What can I do to improve this situation?" This shift in focus empowers you to take proactive steps to address challenges.
- **Practice Gratitude**: As discussed in the previous chapter, practicing gratitude can help maintain a positive outlook. Regularly acknowledging the positive aspects of your life and business can counterbalance the stress of challenges, reinforcing your resilience.

As we conclude this chapter on building resilience, it's paramount to recognize that resilience is a skill that can be developed and strengthened over time. By adopting the strategies outlined—cultivating a growth mindset, developing coping skills, establishing a strong support network, learning from setbacks, setting clear goals, and embracing optimism— you equip yourself to weather the storms of entrepreneurship. Resilience enables you to navigate the inevitable challenges that arise in your journey, allowing you to bounce back, adapt, and continue moving forward. Remember that every setback presents a unique opportunity for growth and learning. The more you practice resilience, the more confident and capable you become in the face of adversity.

Your journey as an entrepreneur is marked by not only the successes you achieve but also your ability to overcome obstacles. By actively building resilience, you position yourself for enduring success that transcends temporary setbacks and propels you toward your long-term vision.

Reflection

Reflect on a recent setback you experienced in your entrepreneurial journey. How did you respond to that challenge? Write down three key takeaways from that experience, along with specific actions you can take to enhance your resilience moving forward. Consider integrating practices such as mindfulness, goal-setting, or seeking support from your network. Commit to fostering resilience in your journey as an entrepreneur, and embrace the strength that comes from overcoming challenges.

Chapter 19
Ethical Entrepreneurship

The importance of integrity and ethics in business practices.

In today's business landscape, the concept of ethical entrepreneurship has gained increasing importance. Today's consumers are not just looking for high-quality products and services; they also prioritize companies that reflect their values and demonstrate integrity in their operations. Ethical entrepreneurship entails conducting business in a manner that is principled, transparent, and socially responsible. In this chapter, we will explore the significance of ethics in entrepreneurship, the benefits of maintaining integrity in business practices, and strategies for implementing ethical principles within your organization.

Understanding Ethical Entrepreneurship

1. **Definition of Ethical Entrepreneurship**: Ethical entrepreneurship refers to the practice of making decisions that align with moral principles and societal values. This encompasses acceptable behaviors such as honesty, fairness, integrity, and

accountability in dealings with customers, employees, suppliers, and the broader community.

2. **The Importance of Ethics**: The importance of ethical entrepreneurship can be summarized through several key dimensions:

   o **Trust Building**: Ethics foster trust between businesses and their stakeholders. Trust is crucial for building long-term relationships with customers, employees, and partners, leading to loyalty and positive word-of-mouth referrals.

   o **Reputation Management**: A strong ethical foundation enhances your brand's reputation. Companies known for their ethical practices are more likely to attract and retain customers, while those with dubious practices risk reputational damage and loss of business.

   o **Social Responsibility**: Ethical entrepreneurship recognizes the impact of business decisions on the community and the environment. By prioritizing social responsibility, entrepreneurs can contribute positively to society while building a sustainable business model.

The Benefits of Ethical Entrepreneurship

1. **Customer Loyalty and Advocacy**: Consumers today are increasingly inclined to support brands that align with their values. By demonstrating a

commitment to ethical practices, you cultivate customer loyalty and encourage advocacy. Loyal customers are more likely to promote your brand within their networks.

2. **Employee Engagement and Retention**: Businesses rooted in ethics tend to attract employees who share similar values. A strong ethical culture enhances employee morale and job satisfaction, resulting in lower turnover rates and increased productivity.

3. **Long-Term Success**: Ethical entrepreneurship is often linked to long-term success. Businesses that prioritize ethical practices create a strong foundation for growth, as they are likely to avoid legal troubles, reputational damage, and operational disruptions caused by unethical behaviors.

4. **Attracting Investment**: Investors are increasingly looking to support ethically responsible businesses. Ethical practices signal sound management and governance, making your company a more attractive investment for ethical investors and venture capitalists.

Strategies for Implementing Ethical Principles

1. Define Core Values and Code of Ethics

Establish clear core values that represent the foundational principles of your business. Create a written code of ethics that outlines the expectations for behavior among employees, management, and partners. This code should address issues such as honesty, integrity, respect, and accountability.

2. Incorporate Ethics into Decision-Making

Make ethical considerations part of your decision-making process. Encourage team members to assess decisions against your core values and code of ethics. When evaluating options, consider how each choice aligns with your organization's commitment to ethical practices.

3. Provide Training and Resources

Educate your team about the importance of ethics and integrity in business practices. Conduct regular training sessions that cover ethical decision-making, compliance, and the implications of unethical behavior. Providing resources, such as a dedicated ethics officer or an internal reporting system for ethical concerns, can empower employees to uphold ethical standards.

4. Encourage Transparency

Transparency is a key component of ethical business practices. Foster open communication both internally and externally. Be honest about your business practices, policies, and performance. When you make mistakes, own up to them, and explain how you will rectify the situation. This transparency builds trust and demonstrates your commitment to ethical responsibility.

5. Engage with the Community

Establish relationships with stakeholders in your community, including customers, suppliers, and local

139

organizations. Involve them in your decision-making processes and seek input on socially responsible initiatives. Engaging with the community helps you understand their needs, fostering a sense of belonging and accountability.

6. **Measure and Evaluate Ethical Practices**

Regularly assess your adherence to ethical practices by establishing metrics and evaluation criteria. Conduct audits, surveys, and feedback sessions to analyze how well you are upholding your ethical commitments. Use these evaluations to make necessary adjustments and maintain accountability throughout your organization.

Real-Life Examples of Ethical Entrepreneurship

1. **Patagonia**: The outdoor apparel company Patagonia is renowned for its commitment to environmental sustainability and social responsibility. Their unique marketing campaigns often promote mindfulness about consumerism and emphasize their mission of reducing environmental impact. By prioritizing sustainability and transparency, Patagonia has built a loyal customer base that advocates for its brand.

2. **Ben & Jerry's**: Known for its commitment to ethical sourcing and environmental responsibility, Ben & Jerry's has made it a priority to focus on fair trade practices and sustainable sourcing in its production processes. The company actively works to ensure that its ingredients are responsibly sourced and has partnered with various organizations to promote environmental and social causes. Their dedication to

ethics in their business model has not only differentiated them in the ice cream industry but has also fostered customer loyalty and engagement.

3. **TOMS Shoes**: TOMS operates on a one-for-one giving model, where for every pair of shoes sold, the company donates a pair to someone in need. This socially conscious approach has positioned TOMS as a leader in ethical entrepreneurship, appealing to consumers who care about social responsibility. Their commitment to giving back has allowed them to cultivate a strong brand identity and a loyal following.

As we conclude this chapter on ethical entrepreneurship, it's clear that integrity and ethical practices are not just optional add-ons for businesses; they are essential to sustainable success. By embedding ethics into the core of your entrepreneurial efforts, you build a foundation that fosters trust, loyalty, and long-term relationships with customers, employees, and communities.

The principles of ethical entrepreneurship guide your decision-making, elevate your brand's reputation, and enhance overall business performance. By implementing the strategies discussed—defining your values, promoting transparency, engaging with the community, and measuring adherence to ethical practices—you position yourself as a leader who prioritizes responsibility and integrity.

As you progress on your entrepreneurial journey, remember that the choices you make today set the tone for the legacy you will leave tomorrow. Strive to build a business that reflects your core values and contributes positively to society. By doing so, you will not only achieve wealth but will create a lasting impact that resonates beyond profits—ultimately leading to a successful and meaningful entrepreneurial journey.

Reflection

Take a moment to consider your current business practices in light of ethical principles. Are there areas where you can strengthen your commitment to ethics and integrity? Write down three specific actions you can take to enhance your ethical practices and align your business with your core values. Whether it's reevaluating your supply chain, improving transparency in communication, or engaging more deeply with your community, commit to making ethical entrepreneurship a central part of your business identity.

Chapter 20
Long-Term Vision and Legacy

Cultivating a vision for lasting impact beyond personal gains.

In the world of entrepreneurship, many individuals are primarily focused on short-term gains—quarters of profit, immediate market competition, and annual revenues. However, the most impactful entrepreneurs understand the importance of cultivating a long-term vision and legacy that extends beyond personal success. A powerful vision guides your business decisions, inspires your team, and leaves a meaningful mark on the industry and community. In this chapter, we will explore the significance of long-term vision, how to cultivate a vision for lasting impact, and the steps necessary to build a legacy that resonates for generations to come.

Understanding Long-Term Vision

1. **Defining Long-Term Vision**: A long-term vision is a clear and compelling picture of where you want your business to be in the future. This vision outlines your core purpose, goals, and the impact you intend to make over time. Unlike short-term goals that may change with market conditions, a long-term vision remains steadfast, serving as a guiding light for your entrepreneurial journey.

2. **The Importance of a Long-Term Vision**:

- Guidance in Decision-Making: A well-articulated vision provides a framework for decision-making. With a clear vision in place, you can evaluate opportunities and challenges against your long-term objectives and values.

- Inspiring Others: A powerful vision motivates and unites your team, stakeholders, and customers. When others understand and believe in your mission, they are more likely to rally behind your initiatives and contribute wholeheartedly to the journey.

- Resilience During Challenges: An inspiring long-term vision serves as a source of motivation during turbulent times. When faced with obstacles or setbacks, reflecting on your vision can help maintain focus and resilience.

Cultivating a Long-Term Vision

1. Reflect on Your Core Values

Start by identifying and reflecting on your core values. What principles guide your decisions? What kind of impact do you want your business to have on society? By grounding your long-term vision in your values, you create an authentic narrative that resonates with all stakeholders, including customers, employees, and partners.

2. Create a Vision Statement

Crafting a concise and compelling vision statement is essential to articulating your long-term goals. This statement should be clear, inspirational, and reflect your aspirations for the future. It serves as a constant reminder of what you are working toward and helps align your team around a shared purpose.

3. **Expand Your Perspective**

When developing your long-term vision, consider the broader implications of your business. Ask yourself:

- How can my business contribute positively to my community and industry?

- What legacy do I want to leave for future entrepreneurs and generations?

- How can I address social, environmental, or economic challenges through my work?

Expanding your perspective will help you form a vision that goes beyond profits and taps into meaningful impact.

4. **Envision the Future**

Take time to visualize the future you aspire to create. Picture your business five, ten, or even twenty years down the line. What does success look like? What kind of culture do you envision? Who are the people impacted by your work? Engaging in this visualization exercise can help clarify your goals and ignite passion for your mission.

Building a Legacy

1. **Commit to Social Responsibility**

Incorporating social responsibility into your long-term vision contributes to a legacy focused on positive impact. Consider how your business can address societal needs, support local communities, or promote sustainability. By committing to ethical practices and social initiatives, you position your business as a force for good.

2. **Mentorship and Knowledge Sharing**

A significant part of building a legacy involves sharing your knowledge and experiences with the next generation of entrepreneurs. Engage in mentorship and offer guidance to aspiring business leaders. This investment in others not only enriches their journeys but also contributes to a culture of growth and collaboration within your industry.

3. **Document Your Journey**

Keep a record of your entrepreneurial journey, including successes, challenges, lessons learned, and reflections on your long-term vision. This documentation serves as a valuable resource for others and can inspire the next wave of entrepreneurs. Consider sharing insights through blogs, books, or speaking engagements, further solidifying your legacy.

4. **Create a Sustainable Business Model**

Focus on building a sustainable business model that can endure beyond your personal involvement. Consider how your company can operate effectively, even in your absence. This may involve developing strong leadership within your team, establishing clear systems and processes, and ensuring your brand's values are embedded in its culture.

As we conclude this chapter on long-term vision and legacy, it is essential to remember that your journey as an entrepreneur extends beyond the here and now. By cultivating a compelling long-term vision, you lay the foundation for a legacy that can inspire, uplift, and create lasting change.

A strong vision will guide your decisions, motivate your team, and attract customers who share your values. Embrace the responsibility that comes with creating a legacy and remain committed to making a positive impact on your community and industry. Remember that the most enduring legacies are built on authenticity, purpose, and a commitment to excellence.

As you venture forward in your entrepreneurial journey, keep your long-term vision at the forefront of your mind. Allow it to inform your daily actions and decisions, and let it inspire those around you. By integrating your values into your business practices and focusing on leaving a positive mark on the world, you create a legacy that goes beyond personal success—one that influences future generations of entrepreneurs.

Reflection

Take this opportunity to reflect on your own long-term vision and the legacy you wish to create. Consider the following questions:

- What impact do you want your business to have on your community and industry?

- What principles and values will guide you on your journey?

- How will you share your knowledge and experiences to uplift others in their entrepreneurial pursuits?

Write down your thoughts and aspirations. Create a detailed vision statement that encapsulates your goals and the legacy you hope to leave behind. By taking these steps, you're not only clarifying your direction but also committing to a path filled with purpose and impact.

Chapter 21

Mentorship: Giving Back

The role of mentorship in personal and professional growth.

In the world of entrepreneurship, success is rarely achieved alone. Behind every successful entrepreneur often stands a network of mentors, advisors, and peers who have provided guidance, support, and valuable insights along the way. Mentorship is a powerful tool for personal and professional growth, creating a cycle of knowledge sharing and investment in the next generation of leaders. In this chapter, we will explore the role of mentorship, its benefits to both mentors and mentees, and actionable strategies for fostering effective mentoring relationships.

Understanding Mentorship

1. **Definition of Mentorship**: Mentorship is a developmental relationship in which a more experienced individual (the mentor) provides guidance, support, and encouragement to a less experienced individual (the mentee). This relationship can take many forms, including one-on-one mentoring, group mentoring, and peer mentoring.

2. **The Importance of Mentorship**: Mentorship plays a vital role in personal and professional development for several reasons:

- o **Knowledge Transfer**: Mentors share their expertise and experiences, providing mentees with insights that can help them navigate challenges and make informed decisions. This transfer of knowledge accelerates learning and skill development.

- o **Networking Opportunities**: Mentors often have extensive networks in their industry. By connecting their mentees with valuable contacts, mentors help broaden their professional opportunities and enhance their visibility within their field.

- o **Confidence Building**: A mentor's support and encouragement can boost a mentee's confidence.. Validation from an experienced individual reassures mentees that they are on the right track and capable of achieving their goals.

- o **Personal Growth**: Mentoring fosters personal growth for both mentors and mentees. Mentors gain a sense of fulfillment by giving back and reflecting on their own journeys, while mentees learn to articulate their goals and aspirations through guided discussions.

The Benefits of Being a Mentor

1. **Giving Back and Creating Impact**: Mentoring provides a fulfilling opportunity to give back to your community and industry. By sharing your knowledge and experiences, you contribute to the development of future entrepreneurs and leaders, leaving a positive impact that extends beyond yourself.

2. **Strengthening Leadership Skills**: Mentoring others offers an opportunity to develop and refine your leadership skills. As a mentor, you are challenged to communicate effectively, listen actively, and provide constructive feedback— essential skills that enhance your own personal and professional growth.

3. **Expanding Your Network**: Mentoring relationships can also benefit mentors by expanding their professional networks. Engaging with eager and motivated mentees allows you to connect with new perspectives and insights, ultimately enriching your understanding of the industry.

4. **Learning from Mentees**: Mentors often find that they learn from their mentees as much as they teach them. Mentees may introduce fresh ideas, approaches, or technologies that challenge mentors to think differently and adapt, fostering a reciprocal learning experience.

The Benefits of Being a Mentee

1. **Guidance and Support**: Having a mentor provides an invaluable source of guidance and support. Near any entrepreneurial challenge, a mentor can offer insights and advice that save you time and resources. Whether you face decisions about navigating a challenging project or scaling a business, their experience becomes a lifeline.

2. **Enhanced Skills and Knowledge**: Mentees benefit from tailored learning experiences. By working closely with a mentor, you can acquire specific skills

and knowledge that are directly relevant to your professional goals, accelerating your growth trajectory.

3. **Increased Accountability**: A mentor serves as an accountability partner. Regular check-ins and discussions with a mentor help you set clear goals and hold you responsible for pursuing them. This accountability encourages you to stay focused and motivated on your path.

4. **Expanding Perspectives**: Mentees gain insights from a seasoned professional who can provide a broader perspective on industry trends, challenges, and opportunities. This expanded viewpoint allows for a more informed approach to problem-solving and decision-making.

Strategies for Fostering Effective Mentorship Relationships

1. Identify Your Mentorship Goals

Before seeking out a mentor or becoming one, take time to define your goals for the relationship. As a mentee, consider what specific skills, knowledge, or insights you want to gain. As a mentor, clarify your intentions in guiding your mentee and the type of impact you want to make.

2. Seek the Right Mentor

When looking for a mentor, identify someone whose expertise aligns with your goals and values. Consider individuals who have experience in the areas you wish to develop. Build a genuine connection with potential mentors and ensure that their guidance and style resonate with you.

3. **Establish Open Communication**

Communication is key to a successful mentorship relationship. Be open about your expectations, needs, and challenges. Schedule regular check-ins to discuss progress, share updates, and seek advice. Foster an environment where both parties feel comfortable discussing challenges and celebrating successes.

4. **Be Receptive to Feedback**

As a mentee, be open to constructive feedback and guidance. Em brace the insights your mentor offers, viewing them as opportunities for growth rather than criticism. Actively seek feedback on your goals, decisions, and progress, and implement suggestions as appropriate. Demonstrating your willingness to learn from their experience will deepen the relationship and enhance your development.

5. **Be Proactive and Engaged**

Mentorship is a two-way street. As a mentee, take the initiative by setting goals for your sessions and coming prepared to discuss your progress and challenges. Demonstrating your commitment and enthusiasm will not only make the relationship more rewarding but also signal to your mentor that their time and guidance are appreciated.

6. **Offer Value as a Mentor**

As a mentor, remember that your relationship with your mentee is not just about imparting knowledge. Show interest in their experiences, ask questions, and listen actively. By valuing their perspective, you create a balanced relationship that fosters mutual respect and trust. Consider sharing opportunities for growth, such as internships or projects, that can help your mentee put their learning into practice.

The Longevity of Mentorship

1. Establish Long-Term Relationships

Effective mentorship relationships can evolve into long-term partnerships that provide ongoing support and guidance throughout your entrepreneurial journey. By fostering these relationships, both parties can continue to benefit from shared experiences and insights.

2. Create a Mentoring Community

Consider establishing a mentoring community within your network or organization. This community can consist of multiple mentors and mentees who cross-share experiences and knowledge. Creating such a platform encourages continuous learning and collaboration among a broader group.

3. Encourage the Next Generation of Mentors

As you grow in your career, inspire your mentees to become mentors themselves. Encourage them to share their knowledge and experiences with others in their network. This cycle of mentorship creates a culture of support and growth within your industry, ensuring that valuable insights are passed down and benefiting future generations of entrepreneurs.

As we conclude this chapter on mentorship, it is important to recognize the profound impact that giving back through mentorship can have on both mentorship and mentees.

Mentorship is a powerful vehicle for personal and professional growth that fosters connection, learning, and empowerment.

Being a mentor allows you to share your journey, impart wisdom, and help shape the next generation of entrepreneurs. Similarly, seeking mentorship opens doors to knowledge, guidance, and opportunities that can significantly enhance your career trajectory.

By actively engaging in the practice of mentorship—whether you're giving or receiving—you create relationships that can lead to transformative experiences. Embrace mentorship as a cornerstone of your entrepreneurial journey, and contribute to a community where knowledge is shared and success is achieved together.

Reflection

Take a moment to reflect on your own experiences with mentorship. Who has influenced you on your journey, and how can you acknowledge their contributions? Consider identifying someone you can reach out to as a potential mentor in your life or contemplate how you can become a mentor to others. Write down three specific actions you will take in the coming weeks to enhance your involvement in mentorship, whether it's seeking a mentor, offering guidance, or building a mentoring community. Commit to the power of mentorship and witness the profound impact it can have on yourself and those around you.

Chapter 22

Creating a Culture of Empowerment

Fostering an environment that encourages innovation and support.

In today's rapidly evolving business landscape, the ability to innovate and adapt is crucial for success. A culture of empowerment plays a pivotal role in fostering an environment where creativity flourishes, employees feel valued, and collaboration thrives. When individuals are empowered, they are more likely to take ownership of their work, contribute innovative ideas, and support one another in their professional journey. In this chapter, we will explore the importance of creating a culture of empowerment, the benefits it brings to your organization, and effective strategies for fostering such an environment.

Understanding Empowerment

1. **Definition of Empowerment**: Empowerment is the process of enabling individuals to take control of their work and make informed decisions. It involves providing the autonomy, resources, and support

necessary for individuals to excel in their roles and contribute to the organization's success.

2. **The Importance of Empowerment**: Cultivating a culture of empowerment has several key benefits:

   ○ **Enhanced Engagement**: When employees feel empowered, they become more engaged and invested in their work. This engagement translates into higher levels of motivation, productivity, and satisfaction.

   ○ **Increased Innovation**: Empowered individuals are more likely to think creatively and propose innovative solutions. By fostering an environment where new ideas are welcome, organizations can drive continuous improvement and stay ahead of the competition.

   ○ **Stronger Team Collaboration**: Empowerment encourages open communication and collaboration among team members. When individuals feel comfortable sharing their ideas and perspectives, it enhances teamwork and strengthens relationships.

   ○ **Improved Retention Rates**: Organizations that prioritize employee empowerment often experience higher retention rates. When employees feel valued and confident in their contributions, they are more likely to stay committed to the organization.

Strategies for Fostering a Culture of Empowerment

1. **Encourage Autonomy**

   Empower employees by granting them autonomy in their roles. Allow individuals the freedom to make decisions and take ownership of their work. This autonomy fosters a sense of responsibility and trust, leading to increased job satisfaction and engagement.

   - **Delegate Responsibilities**: Clearly define roles and responsibilities, and give employees the authority to make decisions within their scope of work. Encourage ownership by letting them lead projects and initiatives.

   - **Avoid Micromanagement**: Resist the urge to micromanage and instead provide support and guidance when needed. Trust your team and allow them to showcase their abilities.

2. **Provide Opportunities for Development**

   Investing in the growth and development of employees is essential for empowerment. Offer training programs, workshops, and resources that help them build their skills and advance their careers. When individuals feel supported in their professional growth, they are more confident and empowered in their roles.

- **Create Personalized Development Plans**: Work with employees to set individual development goals that align with their interests and capabilities. Tailor training opportunities to their needs and aspirations.

- **Mentorship Programs**: Establish formal mentorship programs that connect less experienced employees with seasoned leaders. Mentorship provides guidance, support, and insights that empower individuals to grow and succeed.

3. **Foster Open Communication**

Create an environment where open communication is encouraged and valued. This involves providing channels for feedback, ideas, and discussions.

- **Regular Check-Ins**: Conduct regular one-on-one meetings and team check-ins to discuss progress and gather feedback. Encourage honest conversations about challenges and progress, assuring employees that their opinions are valued.

- **Create Feedback Channels**: Implement platforms for anonymous feedback, suggestion boxes, or surveys to give employees a voice. Incorporate their suggestions into decision-making processes when possible.

4. **Celebrate Achievements and Innovations**

Recognizing and celebrating individual and team successes reinforces a culture of empowerment. Acknowledgment fosters a sense of belonging and encourages employees to continue contributing their best efforts.

- **Implement Recognition Programs**: Create formal recognition programs to celebrate employee achievements, whether big or small. Recognize innovative ideas and implement them within the organization.

- **Share Success Stories**: Highlight success stories within the organization to inspire others. Sharing examples of empowered employees who took initiative and made a difference encourages a culture of innovation.

5. **Encourage Risk-Taking and Learning from Failure**

Empowering employees means creating a safe space where they feel comfortable taking risks without fear of repercussions. Encourage experimentation and embrace the idea that failure is often a stepping stone to success.

- **Promote a Learning Mindset**: Establish a culture that views failures as learning opportunities. Encourage employees to share their experiences and insights from setbacks, reinforcing the lesson that growth comes from trials.

- **Support Innovative Projects**: Dedicate resources to support new projects and initiatives, even if they are high-risk. Encourage teams to experiment and explore new ideas, fostering a culture of innovation.

The Long-Term Impact of an Empowered Culture

1. **Sustainable Innovation**: A culture of empowerment leads to sustainable innovation, where employees consistently contribute fresh ideas, optimize processes, and embrace change. This commitment to continuous improvement keeps the organization competitive in a rapidly evolving market.
2. **Enhanced Employee Satisfaction**: When employees feel empowered, engaged, and valued, their job satisfaction significantly increases. This heightened satisfaction translates into greater productivity, improved morale, and a positive workplace culture that attracts top talent.
3. **Stronger Organizational Resilience**: Empowered employees are more adaptable and resilient in the face of challenges. When the unexpected occurs, they are better equipped to respond proactively, collaborate, and innovate—helping the organization weather storms more effectively.
4. **Positive Community Impact**: An empowered workforce often extends their commitment to social responsibility and community engagement. As individuals feel a sense of agency and responsibility, they are more likely to participate in initiatives that benefit the broader community. This can create a

positive feedback loop that amplifies the organization's impact beyond its immediate business goals.

As we conclude this chapter on creating a culture of empowerment, it's evident that fostering an environment that encourages innovation and support is not only beneficial for your employees but also critical for the long-term success of your organization. Empowerment creates a thriving ecosystem where individuals are motivated to take initiative, share ideas, and collaborate toward common goals.

Investing time and resources into building this culture requires intentional actions, such as promoting autonomy, providing development opportunities, fostering open communication, and celebrating successes. The benefits of implementing these strategies range from enhanced innovation to improved employee satisfaction and community impact.

As you move forward in your entrepreneurial journey, embrace the responsibility of cultivating a culture of empowerment within your organization. By doing so, you empower not only your team but also yourself, creating an environment where everyone can thrive and achieve greatness together.

Reflection

Take a moment to reflect on the current culture within your organization or team. Do you feel that empowerment is a core value? Write down three specific actions you can take to enhance the culture of empowerment in your work environment. Consider how you can promote autonomy, support professional development, or celebrate individual and team achievements. Commit to these actions and observe the positive changes they bring to your organization.

Chapter 23

The Omnipresence of Impact

Understanding the broader impact of your entrepreneurial efforts.

As entrepreneurs, our actions reverberate beyond the walls of our businesses, affecting the lives of our customers, communities, and even future generations. The concept of "omnipresence of impact" reflects the understanding that the influence of our entrepreneurial efforts is pervasive and far-reaching. This chapter will explore how to recognize and cultivate the broader impact of your work, the responsibilities that come with that impact, and actionable strategies to ensure your entrepreneurial journey contributes positively to society.

Understanding the Broader Impact of Entrepreneurship

1. **Economic Contribution**: Entrepreneurs play a crucial role in driving economic growth. By creating jobs, fostering innovation, and contributing to local and global economies, entrepreneurs help stimulate progress and improve living standards. Understanding this economic impact serves as a reminder of the responsibility that comes with running a business.

2. **Social Change**: Many entrepreneurs are motivated by a desire to create social change. Businesses

rooted in social responsibility can address systemic issues such as inequality, environmental degradation, or access to education and healthcare. As an entrepreneur, recognizing the potential for social impact empowers you to create products or services that improve lives.

3. **Cultural Influence**: Entrepreneurship also shapes culture. The values and principles embedded in your business practices influence not just customers, but also employees, communities, and even competitors. By promoting ethical behavior, sustainability, and inclusivity, you contribute to cultural shifts that resonate far and wide.

4. **Environmental Responsibility**: The impact of business practices on the environment is a pressing concern in today's world. Entrepreneurs have the opportunity—and responsibility—to implement sustainable practices that minimize harm to the planet. Recognizing this impact encourages mindful decision-making in operations, sourcing, and production methods.

Recognizing Your Impact

1. **Assessing Your Business Practices**: Take time to evaluate how your business operations contribute to or detract from your local and global environments. Consider questions such as:

   o What materials are used in your products or services?

   o How are employees treated and compensated?

- o Does your business contribute to economic inequality or promote local job growth?

By conducting a thorough assessment, you can gain insights into areas for improvement and opportunities for making a positive impact.

2. **Engaging with Your Community**: Actively participate in your community to better understand its needs and challenges. Engage with local organizations, attend community meetings, and seek input from members of your community. This engagement allows you to identify ways your business can contribute meaningfully.

3. **Gathering Feedback**:Solicit feedback from customers, employees, and stakeholders to gain insights into their perceptions of your business's impact. Understanding how your work is viewed beyond the scope of transactions can reveal areas where you are making a difference—or where there is room for growth.

Strategies to Enhance Your Omnipresence of Impact

1. Establish Social Responsibility Goals

Define clear social responsibility goals that align with your overall mission. These could range from sustainability initiatives and community engagement projects to fair labor practices and ethical sourcing. Setting these goals allows you to create a framework for measuring and enhancing your impact over time.

2. Implement Sustainable Practices

Consider adopting sustainable business practices that prioritize environmental responsibility. This can include sourcing materials from eco-friendly suppliers, reducing waste through recycling or upcycling, and minimizing energy consumption. By integrating sustainability into your operations, you show your commitment to the planet and contribute positively to its health.

3. **Create Partnerships for Impact**

Collaborate with organizations, nonprofits, and other businesses that share your commitment to making a positive impact. Partnerships can amplify your efforts and reach, allowing you to leverage the strengths and resources of others in your mission to drive change.

4. **Engage Employees in Impact Initiatives**

Encourage your team to get involved in initiatives that promote social responsibility and community engagement. Create programs that allow employees to volunteer their time or contribute to charitable efforts. By empowering your workforce to participate in impact initiatives, you foster a shared sense of purpose and commitment to making a difference.

5. **Communicate Your Impact**

Share your efforts to create a positive impact with your customers and stakeholders. Transparently communicate your goals, the initiatives you are implementing, and the results you are achieving. This communication not only builds trust but also encourages others to consider how they can contribute to similar efforts.

Reflecting on Your Legacy

1. **Consider the Long-Term Effects**: As you build your business, frequently reflect on the long-term effects of your actions. What kind of legacy do you hope to leave behind? Think deeply about the values and principles that will define your organization in the future.

2. **Encourage Future Leaders**: Share your journey and experiences with the next generation of entrepreneurs. By mentoring budding entrepreneurs, you pass down valuable lessons and inspire them to consider the broader impact of their work.

3. **Create a Culture of Impact**: Foster an organizational culture that prioritizes impact. Encourage ongoing conversations about how your team can contribute to positive change and continuously seek new opportunities to enhance your impact.

As we conclude this chapter on the omnipresence of impact, it's vital to recognize that as entrepreneurs, the influence of our choices extends far beyond the immediate sphere of our businesses. Each decision we make affects not only our customers and employees but also the communities and environments within which we operate.

Cultivating an awareness of the broader implications of your entrepreneurial efforts empowers you to make responsible choices that contribute positively to society. By embracing ethical practices, prioritizing sustainability, and engaging with your community, you can create a legacy that reflects your values and makes a lasting difference.

Make it your mission to see opportunities for impact in every aspect of your work. From the products you develop to the relationships you build, you have the power to initiate change and inspire others to do the same. Remember that creating a positive impact requires commitment and intentionality, but the rewards—both for your business and for the greater good—are immeasurable.

Reflection

Take a moment to reflect on your current understanding of impact and how it relates to your entrepreneurial journey. Consider the following questions:

- What impact do you hope your business will have on others and the environment?
- How can you align your business practices with your values to create a positive influence?
- What specific actions can you take in the coming weeks to enhance your impact within your community or industry?

Write down your thoughts and commitments. By consciously developing an impact-driven approach to your business, you contribute to a more sustainable and ethical future for yourself and the next generation of entrepreneurs.

Chapter 24

Pioneering Change

How entrepreneurs can lead social and industry change.

Entrepreneurs have always played a pivotal role in driving social and industry change. Beyond their pursuit of profit, many are motivated by the desire to create solutions to societal challenges, improve lives, and disrupt outdated practices. Pioneering change involves understanding the dynamics of your industry, leveraging innovation, and actively working towards solutions that benefit both the market and the community. In this chapter, we will explore how entrepreneurs can lead transformative change, the strategies they can employ, and inspiring examples of entrepreneurs who have made a significant impact.

The Role of Entrepreneurs in Driving Change

1. **Innovators and Disruptors**: Entrepreneurs are often seen as innovators who challenge the status quo. By introducing new ideas, products, or services, they have the unique ability to disrupt existing markets and create entirely new industries. This innovation is the catalyst for change, pushing boundaries and reshaping sectors.

2. **Navigators of Shifts**: In a rapidly evolving world, entrepreneurs can quickly respond to societal and technological changes. They possess the agility needed to adapt to shifting needs and embrace

emerging trends, which positions them as key players in leading industry transformations.

3. **Moral and Ethical Leaders**: Many entrepreneurs recognize the importance of corporate social responsibility and strive to implement ethical practices within their businesses. By prioritizing social and environmental considerations, they pave the way for a more sustainable future and inspire others to follow suit.

Strategies for Pioneering Change

1. Develop a Clear Vision for Change

To effectively lead change, you must have a clear vision of what you want to achieve. This vision should outline the specific changes you seek to implement, the impact you hope to create, and the values that will guide your efforts.

- **Articulate Your Purpose**: Define and communicate the purpose behind your vision for change. Explain why it matters and how it fits within the larger context of your industry or society. This clarity will help rally support from stakeholders, employees, and customers.

2. Engage Stakeholders

Pioneering change requires the support and collaboration of stakeholders across various levels. Engage with employees, customers, industry peers, community members, and local organizations to build a coalition for change.

- **Foster Collaboration**: Collaborate with others who share your vision or have complementary goals.

Whether through partnerships, strategic alliances, or community initiatives, collective efforts magnify impact and facilitate deeper change.

3. **Leverage Technology and Innovation**

Technology can be a powerful driver of change. Identify ways to incorporate new technologies into your business model that align with your vision and can create more efficient, sustainable, or transformative solutions.

- **Stay Informed**: Keep abreast of technological advancements and market trends relevant to your industry. Innovate with these insights in mind to develop products and services that fundamentally improve the existing landscape.

4. **Advocate for Policy Changes**

As entrepreneurs, you have the opportunity to advocate for policy changes that align with your vision of a better future. Engage with stakeholders and policymakers to propose regulations, initiatives, or reforms that advance social or industry issues you care about.

- **Participate in Industry Associations**: Join associations or coalitions that focus on policy change in your industry. Collaborate with other entrepreneurs to present a unified voice advocating for meaningful change.

5. **Embrace a Culture of Experimentation**

Pioneering change involves taking risks and being willing to experiment. Encourage a culture of innovation within your organization, where employees feel empowered to propose new ideas and solutions without fear of failure.

- **Pilot Programs**: Test new initiatives or solutions through pilot programs. Gather feedback to refine your approach, demonstrating a commitment to learning and adapting as you pursue your vision.

Inspiring Examples of Entrepreneurs Leading Change

1. **Elon Musk (Tesla and SpaceX)**: Elon Musk is a prime example of an entrepreneur who has pioneered change across multiple industries. With Tesla, he has revolutionized the automotive industry by pushing the limits of electric vehicle technology and sustainability. At SpaceX, Musk aims to decrease the cost of space travel and make it accessible to the masses. His vision has inspired a new direction for both the automotive industry and space exploration.

2. **Blake Mycoskie (TOMS Shoes)**: Blake Mycoskie founded TOMS Shoes with a mission to tackle the issue of global poverty through the "One for One" model, where for every pair of shoes sold, a pair is donated to those in need. His commitment to social responsibility has transformed the footwear industry and inspired countless other brands to implement socially conscious practices.

3. **Yvon Chouinard (Patagonia)**: Patagonia is a leader in environmental activism and responsible business practices. Yvon Chouinard, the company's founder, has consistently used his platform to advocate for environmental sustainability and the protection of natural resources. By prioritizing ethical

sourcing, community engagement, and activism, Patagonia has become a model for how businesses can impact society positively.

As we conclude this chapter on pioneering change, it's essential to recognize that, as an entrepreneur, you have the power to shape not just your business but also the world around you. Embracing your role as a change leader means understanding the significant impact of your work and utilizing it to create positive outcomes for individuals, communities, and industries.

Leading change requires vision, determination, and the willingness to take bold steps. By developing a clear vision, engaging stakeholders, leveraging technology, advocating for policy changes, and fostering a culture of experimentation, you can effectively pioneer change in your organization and industry. Remember that every effort, no matter how small, contributes to meaningful progress.

The journey of pioneering change is continuous; it requires patience, resilience, and adaptability. As market dynamics evolve and new challenges arise, staying committed to your vision will guide you through uncertainty. Be inspired by trailblazers who have come before you, and allow their stories to fuel your own efforts to innovate and lead.

As you move forward in your entrepreneurial journey, continually ask yourself: What change do I want to see in the world? How can my business make a difference? By keeping these questions in focus, you can align your efforts with a greater purpose and inspire others to join you in creating a better future.

Reflection

Take a moment to reflect on your vision for change. What specific changes do you hope to bring about within your industry or community? Write down your thoughts on how you can leverage your entrepreneurial efforts to lead initiatives that promote positive impact. Identify three actionable steps you can take in the coming weeks to start pioneering this change — whether it's through advocacy, collaboration, or innovative practices. Commit to being a force for change and embrace the responsibility of shaping a better world through your entrepreneurial endeavors.

Chapter 25

Your Unique Journey

Celebrating the individual paths of entrepreneurs.

Every entrepreneur has a unique journey, shaped by personal experiences, challenges, aspirations, and milestones. This individuality is one of the most powerful aspects of the entrepreneurial spirit. Understanding and embracing your unique journey not only helps you navigate the often turbulent waters of entrepreneurship but also allows you to celebrate your personal achievements and lessons learned along the way. In this chapter, we will explore the importance of recognizing your unique journey, the stories that define your path, and strategies to honor and leverage these experiences to foster growth in yourself and your business.

The Importance of Celebrating Individual Journeys

1. **Embracing Individuality**: Each entrepreneur comes from a different background, culture, and experience. Embracing your individuality enables you to leverage your strengths and perspectives in pursuit of your goals. It recognizes that there is no single formula for success and that your unique qualities can set you apart in a competitive landscape.

2. **Learning from Experiences**: Your journey is filled with valuable lessons learned from successes and failures. Celebrating your experiences allows you to reflect on these lessons, understand their impact,

and apply the knowledge gained in future endeavors. Each step you take contributes to your overall growth as an entrepreneur.

3. **Inspiring Others**: Sharing your unique journey has the potential to inspire others facing similar challenges. Your story can resonate with aspiring entrepreneurs who may see themselves in your experiences. Celebrating and sharing your path fosters a sense of community and motivation, encouraging others to pursue their own dreams.

4. **Building Resilience**: Acknowledging the ups and downs of your journey increases resilience. Understanding that setbacks are a natural part of the entrepreneurial experience helps you maintain a positive outlook and reinforces your capacity to overcome future challenges.

Recognizing Your Unique Path

1. **Reflect on Your Origins**: Take time to reflect on your background and what inspired you to become an entrepreneur. What experiences shaped your perspective? Did you encounter particular challenges that motivated you to pursue your goals? Consider crafting a personal narrative that encapsulates your journey, helping you connect your past with your present ambitions.

2. **Identify Pivotal Moments**: Throughout your journey, certain moments likely stand out as turning points—both positive and negative. Identify these pivotal experiences and examine how they influenced your decisions and shaped your path.

Recognizing these moments helps you understand the trajectory of your journey and enhances your ability to extract lessons from them.

3. **Celebrate Milestones**: As you progress in your entrepreneurial journey, celebrate milestones along the way. Whether achieving a significant sales target, launching a new product, or completing a challenging project, acknowledging these accomplishments reinforces your growth and instills confidence for future endeavors.

Sharing Your Story

1. **Engage with Your Community**: Sharing your story with others cultivates connections and inspires those who may have similar aspirations. Use community platforms, social media, or networking events to discuss your journey and the experiences that define it. Engaging with your audience allows you to create a support network and foster relationships that encourage growth.

2. **Write or Speak About Your Journey**: Consider documenting your story in a blog, book, or public speaking event. Articulating your experiences not only serves to inspire others but also allows for self-reflection and deeper understanding of what you have accomplished. Your insights can provide valuable guidance to emerging entrepreneurs navigating their own journeys.

3. **Leverage Your Unique Experiences in Branding**: Use your unique journey as a foundation for your

brand identity. Infuse aspects of your personal story into your brand messaging, mission statement, and marketing efforts. Authenticity resonates with customers, and sharing your journey can enhance emotional connections with your audience.

The Impact of Your Journey on Others

1. **Mentorship and Community Building**: As you embrace and celebrate your unique journey, consider how you can give back to your community or mentor those who are just starting their entrepreneurial paths. Sharing your insights and experiences can provide valuable guidance and encouragement, creating a culture of support and empowerment.

2. **Encouraging Diverse Perspectives**: By honoring individual journeys, you create a space that values diverse perspectives and experiences. Celebrate the stories of others within your team or network, recognizing that everyone has unique contributions to make. Fostering inclusivity and supporting diverse entrepreneurial pathways enriches the ecosystem and drives innovation.

3. **Leaving a Legacy**: Your journey contributes to a larger narrative—one that can resonate and inspire future generations of entrepreneurs. Reflect on the legacy you wish to leave behind. What values and lessons do you want to impart? Consider how your

experiences can shape the aspirations of future innovators and create a lasting impact.

In conclusion, celebrating your unique journey is essential for both personal growth and the broader entrepreneurial community. Every experience, whether a triumph or a setback, contributes to the tapestry of your entrepreneurial identity. By recognizing, reflecting upon, and sharing your story, you empower yourself and others to thrive in the ever-evolving world of entrepreneurship.

Embrace your individuality and the journey that comes with it. Accept that your path may be different from others, and that is precisely what makes you unique and valuable in your field. Your experiences are a treasure trove of insights that can serve as guidance, inspiration, and support not only for yourself but also for those who learn from you.

As you move forward, remember that the journey of entrepreneurship is as important as the destination. Celebrate the milestones, learn from the challenges, and continue to evolve. Embrace the impact of your story—not just on your life, but on those around you, as your journey has the power to ignite passion and motivation in others.

Reflection

Take a moment to reflect on your unique entrepreneurial journey. Consider the underlying experiences that have shaped your path and the lessons you have learned along the way. Write down a personal narrative that highlights key moments, challenges, and successes in your journey. Identify three actions you can take to share your story with others—whether through mentoring, public speaking, or content creation. By acknowledging and celebrating your journey, you contribute to a community built on shared experiences and collective encouragement.

Chapter 26
The Road Ahead

Preparing for future challenges and opportunities.

As an entrepreneur, navigating the unpredictable landscape of business can often feel like driving through a winding road with hills and valleys, sharp turns and unexpected detours. Preparing for future challenges and opportunities is essential for success in this dynamic environment. A proactive mindset, combined with strategic planning, equips you to not only overcome obstacles but also seize emerging opportunities as they arise. In this chapter, we will explore the importance of foresight in entrepreneurship, strategies for preparing for the future, and how to cultivate an adaptive mindset that embraces change.

The Importance of Foresight

1. **Anticipating Changes**: The business landscape is constantly evolving, influenced by trends, technology, consumer behavior, and economic shifts. Foresight enables entrepreneurs to anticipate changes and prepare for them ahead of time rather than merely reacting after the fact.

2. **Strategic Planning**: With foresight, you can develop a long-term strategic plan that outlines your vision, objectives, and the steps needed to achieve them. This planning provides a roadmap that keeps you aligned with your goals while allowing room for adjustments as the landscape shifts.

3. **Risk Mitigation**: Understanding potential challenges helps you develop strategies to mitigate risks. This proactive approach reduces the chances of experiencing negative impacts and positions your business to withstand adversity.

Strategies for Preparing for Future Challenges and Opportunities

1. Conduct Environmental Scanning

Regularly engage in environmental scanning to identify trends, threats, and opportunities relevant to your industry. This process involves analyzing market dynamics, technological advancements, and consumer behavior.

- **Stay Informed**: Subscribing to industry publications, attending conferences, and joining professional organizations can provide valuable insights into emerging trends. Consider dedicating time each week to research and stay attuned to shifts that may impact your business.

2. Embrace Innovation

Innovation is a critical component of long-term success. Continually explore ways to improve your products, services, and processes. Encourage a culture of creativity within your team, empowering them to generate new ideas and solutions.

- **Invest in R&D**: Allocate resources for research and development initiatives, as these can lead to breakthroughs that enhance your offerings and keep you ahead of the curve.

3. Set Flexible Goals

While having clear goals is crucial, it's equally important to maintain flexibility in your plans. Setting adaptable goals allows you to pivot as new information and opportunities arise. Implement a framework that encourages regular review and adjustment of your objectives based on market conditions.

- **Use OKRs**: Consider implementing Objectives and Key Results (OKRs) to set flexible yet measurable goals that align with your vision and help you quickly adapt to changes.

4. **Develop Contingency Plans**

Contingency planning involves preparing for potential setbacks or crises. Identify possible challenges that could arise and outline specific actions to address them. Having a response plan in place allows you to act quickly and effectively when challenges occur.

- **Scenario Planning**: Engage in scenario planning exercises by envisioning various possible futures based on different variables (economic downturns, industry disruptions, etc.). Create action plans for each scenario, ensuring you're ready no matter what the future holds.

5. **Cultivate a Learning Organization**

Building a culture of continuous learning within your organization helps prepare you for future challenges. Encourage team members to pursue professional development, stay updated on industry advancements, and share knowledge.

- **Training Programs**: Offer training, workshops, and resources that empower employees to enhance their skills. This investment not only prepares your team for future demands but strengthens your organization as a whole.

Developing an Adaptive Mindset

1. Embrace Change as an Opportunity

Cultivating an adaptive mindset means viewing change as an opportunity for growth rather than a threat. Embracing change fosters resilience and innovation, allowing you to navigate uncertainties with confidence.

- **Practice Flexibility**: When faced with unexpected challenges, remain open to adaptation. Assess the situation and consider alternative strategies that align with your long-term vision.

2. Seek Feedback and Input

Involve your team in discussions about potential challenges and opportunities. Engage in open dialogues that encourage feedback and diverse perspectives. This inclusive approach helps promote an adaptive culture where everyone feels empowered to contribute.

- **Regular Team Meetings**: Hold regular brainstorming sessions or strategy meetings to gather insights and ideas from your team about how to address challenges and explore new opportunities.

3. Cultivate Resilience

While preparing for future challenges, focus on developing your resilience as an entrepreneur. Build emotional resilience by practicing self-care, maintaining a support network, and developing coping strategies for stress.

- **Mindfulness Practices**: Incorporate mindfulness techniques, such as meditation or journaling, into your routine to enhance self-awareness and nurture a positive mindset. A resilient entrepreneur is better equipped to handle the pressures and uncertainties that come with their journey.

As we conclude this chapter on preparing for future challenges and opportunities, it is essential to recognize that the entrepreneurial journey is a continuous evolution marked by change and adaptation. By embracing a proactive approach to foresight, innovation, and adaptability, you position yourself and your business to thrive in an unpredictable landscape.

The road ahead may be filled with challenges, but with the right strategies, an open mindset, and a commitment to continuous improvement, you will foster an environment of resilience and preparedness. Remember, successful entrepreneurs do not merely react to obstacles; they anticipate them and adapt their strategies accordingly.

By creating flexible plans, cultivating a culture of learning, and maintaining an unwavering focus on your long-term vision, you will not only weather storms but emerge stronger and more capable of navigating future uncertainties.

As you move forward in your entrepreneurial journey, remain vigilant and curious. Continuously seek out opportunities for growth and innovation, and be willing to pivot when necessary. The future is full of potential, and your ability to adapt and grow will dictate your success.

Reflection

Take a moment to reflect on your current readiness for future challenges and opportunities. What aspects of your business might require more foresight and adaptability? Write down three specific actions you can implement to enhance your preparedness for the road ahead—whether it's conducting regular market assessments, creating contingency plans, or investing in skills development for your team. Commit to taking these actions to ensure you are well-equipped to embrace the challenges and opportunities that lie on your entrepreneurial journey.

Chapter 27
Wisdom from the Field

Lessons learned from other entrepreneurs and their stories.

Throughout the entrepreneurial journey, one of the most valuable resources available to aspiring and established entrepreneurs alike is the wealth of knowledge shared through the experiences of others. In this chapter, we will explore the powerful lessons learned from successful entrepreneurs, highlighting their stories, insights, and the wisdom they impart. By learning from the triumphs and tribulations of others, you can better navigate your own path and avoid common pitfalls.

Learning from Real-World Experiences

1. **Valuable Insights**: Entrepreneurs operate in dynamic environments filled with challenges and opportunities. By sharing their personal experiences, successful entrepreneurs offer valuable insights into what works and what doesn't, helping others navigate similar situations with greater awareness.

2. **Resilience and Adaptability**: Many stories of successful entrepreneurs are defined by their ability to adapt to changing circumstances and overcome setbacks. These narratives serve as reminders that resilience is paramount in entrepreneurship. Witnessing how others faced adversity can instill

hope and motivation during challenging times in your own journey.

3. **Innovation and Creativity**: The entrepreneurial landscape is rich with examples of innovation born out of necessity. By studying the stories of inventive entrepreneurs, you can spark your creativity and inspire your approach to problem-solving.

Lessons Learned from Notable Entrepreneurs

1. Howard Schultz (Starbucks)

Howard Schultz's journey to transforming Starbucks into a global brand is a testament to the importance of customer experience and company culture. Schultz entered Starbucks when it was a small coffee bean retailer, but after traveling to Italy and experiencing the coffee culture, he envisioned a welcoming café experience for customers.

Key Lesson: **Prioritize the Customer Experience** Schultz focused on creating an inviting atmosphere where customers felt at home, making Starbucks more than just a coffee shop. This emphasis on customer experience became a cornerstone of Starbucks' brand identity, demonstrating that a business's success is deeply tied to how well it serves and engages with its customers.

2. Richard Branson (Virgin Group)

Richard Branson, founder of the Virgin Group, is known for his adventurous spirit and willingness to challenge conventional wisdom. His journey exemplifies the power of brand diversification and risk-taking. Branson ventured into various industries, from music to airlines to space tourism, often pursuing ideas that others deemed impossible.

Key Lesson: Embrace Risk and Adventure
Branson's story emphasizes the significance of taking calculated risks and being willing to step outside one's comfort zone. It encourages aspiring entrepreneurs to challenge the status quo and pursue unconventional ideas, as they may lead to remarkable breakthroughs and new business opportunities.

3. **Sara Blakely (Spanx)**

Sara Blakely, the founder of Spanx, built an empire from a simple idea for shapewear. Blakely began her journey with a small amount of savings and a determination to solve a problem she saw in women's clothing. She faced numerous rejections from manufacturers and retailers but remained steadfast in her vision.

Key Lesson: Persistence Pays Off
Blakely's story illustrates the importance of persistence in entrepreneurship. Her unwavering dedication to her idea, despite facing challenges, ultimately led to her success. She also emphasizes that failure is a part of the journey; believing in oneself and persevering through adversity can lead to incredible achievements.

4. **Elon Musk (Tesla and SpaceX)**

Elon Musk's entrepreneurial journey is characterized by his ambitious vision for the future. With Tesla, he aims to accelerate the world's transition to sustainable energy, while SpaceX seeks to make space travel accessible and eventually enable colonization of other planets. Musk's relentless pursuit of innovation has pushed boundaries in multiple industries.

Key Lesson: Think Big and Aim High
Musk's visionary mindset encourages entrepreneurs to set audacious goals and tackle significant challenges. By thinking big and aspiring to solve the world's pressing problems, entrepreneurs can create meaningful change and impact. His approach emphasizes that even the most ambitious dreams are worth pursuing.

5. Randi Zuckerberg (Zuckerberg Media)

Randi Zuckerberg, founder of Zuckerberg Media and former director of market development at Facebook, uses her platform to encourage creativity and innovation. After leaving Facebook, she explored her passion for storytelling through various mediums, including writing, television, and her entrepreneurial endeavors.

Key Lesson: Embrace Creativity and Diversification
Zuckerberg's story highlights the importance of embracing creativity in multiple forms. She encourages entrepreneurs to explore their passions and diversify their skills. Leveraging creative talents can lead to unique opportunities and richer professional experiences.

Strategies for Extracting Wisdom from Others

1. Build a Network of Diverse Entrepreneurs

Broaden your network to include entrepreneurs from various backgrounds and industries. Diversity in your connections can provide you with a wide range of perspectives and insights, enriching your understanding of different approaches.

2. Engage in Mentorship

Seek mentorship from experienced entrepreneurs or industry leaders. A mentor can offer guidance, share relevant stories, and provide invaluable knowledge gained from their experiences.

Read Biographies and Case Studies Delve into biographies and case studies of successful entrepreneurs. These resources often provide in-depth insights into the journeys of notable figures, detailing their challenges, triumphs, and the lessons they learned along the way. This literature can be a rich source of inspiration and practical knowledge.

4. **Attend Workshops and Conferences**

Participate in events, workshops, and conferences where successful entrepreneurs share their insights and stories. Engaging in such environments not only allows you to learn from their experiences but also gives you the opportunity to network and connect with like-minded individuals who share your aspirations.

5. **Share Your Own Experiences**

As you gather knowledge from others, also be willing to share your own entrepreneurial journey. By sharing your successes and failures, you contribute to the collective wisdom and help inspire the next generation of entrepreneurs. Engaging in conversations about your experiences fosters a sense of community and collaboration.

As we conclude this chapter on wisdom from the field, it is essential to recognize that the journey of entrepreneurship is a continuous learning process. The insights gained from the experiences of others can significantly enrich your understanding of the challenges and opportunities you will encounter on your path.

Embracing a mindset of learning from the stories of successful entrepreneurs enables you to navigate your unique journey with greater confidence and awareness. By incorporating their lessons—whether it's about perseverance, embracing innovation, or prioritizing customer experience—you can forge your own path while avoiding common pitfalls.

As you move forward in your entrepreneurial endeavors, prioritize learning from those who have walked the path before you. Let their wisdom guide you, inspire you, and inform your decisions. By doing so, you not only enhance your chances of success but also contribute to a culture of shared knowledge and support within the entrepreneurial community.

Reflection

Reflect on the entrepreneurs whose journeys resonate with you. What specific lessons have you learned from their experiences that you can apply to your journey? Write down three entrepreneurs you admire and summarize the valuable insights you can extract from their stories. Additionally, think about how you can share your own experiences to help and inspire others on their paths. Commit to engaging with the entrepreneurial community and fostering a culture of learning and mentorship as you continue your journey.

Chapter 28

The Heart of Entrepreneurship

Capturing passion and purpose in every endeavor.

At its core, entrepreneurship is a journey fueled by passion and purpose. It is not merely about creating a product or service; it is about solving problems, making an impact, and pursuing a vision that resonates deeply with the entrepreneur's values and beliefs. This chapter will explore the significance of capturing passion and purpose in every entrepreneurial endeavor, how these elements drive motivation and innovation, and practical strategies for aligning your business with your intrinsic motivations.

Understanding Passion and Purpose

1. **Defining Passion**: Passion is the intense enthusiasm or love for what you do. It drives entrepreneurs to invest time, energy, and resources into their business endeavors, often pushing them to go above and beyond in pursuing their goals. When you are passionate about your work, it becomes a source of joy, fulfillment, and inspiration.

2. **Defining Purpose**: Purpose goes beyond passion; it encompasses the deeper reason for your business's existence. Purpose is your "why"—the impact you seek to make on your customers, industry, and the world. A strong sense of purpose

provides direction and meaning, guiding your decisions and actions in alignment with your vision.

The Power of Passion and Purpose

1. **Driving Motivation**: Passion and purpose are powerful motivators that keep entrepreneurs energized, even during challenging times. When the road gets tough, revisiting your reasons for starting your journey can rekindle your enthusiasm and commitment.

2. **Inspiring Others**: A clear sense of purpose inspires not only you but also your team, customers, and stakeholders. When others see your passion and dedication to making a difference, they are more likely to rally around your vision and contribute meaningfully to your goals.

3. **Facilitating Resilience**: A strong connection to your passion and purpose enhances your ability to persevere through setbacks and challenges. With a clear understanding of what drives you, you are more likely to view obstacles as stepping stones rather than roadblocks. This resilience is essential for long-term success.

4. **Enhancing Creativity and Innovation**: Passionate entrepreneurs often think outside the box, finding creative solutions to problems and innovating within their industries. When you are genuinely interested in what you do, you're more likely to explore new

ideas and take calculated risks that can lead to groundbreaking developments.

Strategies for Infusing Passion and Purpose in Your Business

1. Reflect on Your "Why"

Take time to reflect on the motivations that drove you to become an entrepreneur. What challenges or problems do you hope to address through your work? What legacy do you aspire to leave? Writing down your thoughts can clarify your purpose and strengthen your resolve.

2. Align Your Business Practices with Your Values

Ensure that your business practices reflect your values and core beliefs. This alignment enhances authenticity and allows you to operate with integrity. When your passion and purpose permeate your operations, employees, customers, and stakeholders can sense this commitment, leading to stronger connections and support.

3. Involve Your Team in Your Vision

Share your passion and purpose with your team, engaging them in discussions about the company's mission and goals. Encourage team members to contribute ideas and insights on how to embody these values in their daily work.

Creating a culture in which everyone feels a sense of ownership over the vision fosters motivation and unity.

4. **Create Impactful Products and Services**

Design your products and services with your passion and purpose in mind. Ask yourself how your offerings can genuinely make a difference in customers' lives or address pressing societal issues. This alignment not only enhances customer satisfaction but also reinforces your commitment to your mission.

5. **Regularly Revisit and Refine Your Purpose**

As your business grows and evolves, it's crucial to periodically revisit your purpose and ensure it remains relevant. Engage in regular self-reflection and involve your team in conversations about how the company's mission aligns with current challenges or opportunities. This practice ensures that your passion and purpose continue to guide your endeavors.

Stories of Passion and Purpose in Entrepreneurship

1. **Brendan Schwartz (Knotty Tie Co.)**: Brendan Schwartz founded Knotty Tie Co. with a mission to provide jobs to refugees and immigrants while promoting sustainability through custom-made ties. His passion for social impact and community-building drives the company's purpose. By aligning his business with his values, Schwartz inspires his team and customers to engage in meaningful social change.

2. **Jessica Herrin (Stella & Dot)**: Jessica Herrin, founder of Stella & Dot, built her fashion brand

around the idea of empowering women to become entrepreneurs. Her personal experiences and dedication to female empowerment drive the company's purpose. Herrin's commitment to providing opportunities for women to thrive in business has resonated throughout the organization, creating a thriving community of independent stylists.

3. **Muhammad Yunus (Grameen Bank)**: Awarded the Nobel Peace Prize, Muhammad Yunus founded Grameen Bank to combat poverty in Bangladesh through micro-lending. His passion for social justice and economic empowerment led to a global movement. Yunus's work illustrates how a deep sense of purpose can drive transformative change. By providing small loans to impoverished individuals, particularly women, he has empowered countless people to start their own businesses, improve their living conditions, and achieve financial independence.

The Lasting Effects of Passion and Purpose

1. **Inspiring Future Generations**: Entrepreneurs who operate with passion and purpose create a ripple effect that inspires others. When you live your mission authentically, you motivate peers, employees, and emerging entrepreneurs to pursue their own dreams with similar zeal and commitment. Your journey can serve as a blueprint for others seeking to make a positive impact.
2. **Building Lasting Relationships**: An organization that embodies passion and purpose naturally attracts like-

minded individuals, customers, and partners. These relationships are often built on shared values, creating a loyal community that supports and amplifies your efforts.
3. **Contributing to a Greater Good**: When entrepreneurs prioritize their passion and purpose, they contribute not just to their own success, but also to the betterment of society as a whole. The collective efforts of purpose-driven entrepreneurs can lead to sustainable innovations, improved communities, and solutions to pressing global challenges.

As we conclude this chapter on the heart of entrepreneurship, it's essential to recognize that passion and purpose are more than just motivational buzzwords; they are powerful forces that can transform your entrepreneurial journey and influence the lives of others. Engaging with your passion and aligning it with a meaningful purpose ensures that your work is fulfilling, impactful, and sustainable.

As you continue on your entrepreneurial path, take the time to cultivate the heart of your business. Reflect on your motivations, articulate your vision, and embed your values into every facet of your operations. By doing so, you not only enhance your own experience but also inspire those around you to engage in the journey with purpose and passion.

Reflection

Take a moment to reflect on your entrepreneurial journey thus far. What drives your passion for your work? What impact do you hope to create through your business? Write down a personal mission statement that encapsulates your values and aspirations. Identify three specific actions you can take in the coming weeks to align your business practices with your passion and purpose. Commit to celebrating your journey and embracing the heart of entrepreneurship as you move forward.

Chapter 29

Staying Relevant in a Changing World

Adapting to ongoing changes and trends in entrepreneurship.

The entrepreneurial landscape is inherently dynamic, characterized by rapid changes in technology, consumer preferences, market trends, and global events. To thrive in this environment, entrepreneurs must develop the ability to adapt swiftly and effectively. Staying relevant is not just about reacting to changes; it involves a proactive approach that continuously anticipates trends, embraces innovation, and aligns strategies with evolving consumer needs. In this chapter, we will explore the importance of maintaining relevance in entrepreneurship, strategies for adapting to change, and how to cultivate a mindset geared toward continuous growth and innovation.

The Importance of Staying Relevant

1. **Market Competitiveness**: In an increasingly competitive environment, staying relevant helps you differentiate your business from competitors. Businesses that fail to adapt risk losing their customer base to those that offer more innovative solutions or respond better to changing needs.

2. **Customer Loyalty**: Consumers are drawn to brands that understand and evolve with their preferences.

By staying relevant, you foster loyalty among your customers, demonstrating that you value their needs and are committed to meeting them.

3. **Sustainability for Growth**: Relevance is closely tied to sustainable growth. Businesses that consistently adapt and innovate are better positioned for long-term success. By staying current, you improve your chances of making informed decisions that lead to successful outcomes.

Strategies for Adapting to Change

1. Commit to Ongoing Learning

Continuous learning is critical for staying relevant in entrepreneurship. Engage in professional development through workshops, seminars, and online courses to keep your skills and knowledge up to date.

- **Industry Trends**: Regularly read industry reports, articles, and publications to remain informed about emerging trends and advancements that can influence your business.

2. Seek Customer Feedback

Engage with your customers regularly to gather insights on their needs, preferences, and experiences. Use surveys, feedback forms, and social media interactions to gain valuable information that can inform your decisions.

- **Iterate Based on Input**: Be open to using customer feedback for iterative improvements. Developing a feedback loop allows you to refine your offerings and align closely with your audience's expectations.

3. Embrace Technological Advancements

Technology is a driving force behind many changes in entrepreneurship. Keep an eye on technological innovations that can enhance your operations, improve efficiency, or create new opportunities.

- **Invest in Tools and Platforms**: Explore tools and platforms that can streamline processes, enhance customer engagement, or enable data-driven decision-making. Adopting the latest technologies can provide you with a competitive edge.

4. Conduct Regular Market Analysis

Consistently analyze your market to identify shifts in consumer behavior and preferences. Utilize market research techniques to understand the overall landscape and what drives your competitors' success.

- **Scenario Planning**: Engage in scenario planning to simulate potential future changes in the market and evaluate how your business can respond effectively. Anticipating scenarios helps you prepare for various possibilities.

5. Cultivate a Flexible Culture

Fostering a culture of flexibility within your organization enables your team to adapt to changes with ease.

Encourage open communication, creativity, and a willingness to experiment with new ideas.

- **Empower Employees**: Give your team the autonomy to explore new approaches and share their insights. Empowering employees fosters a sense of ownership and inspires them to contribute actively to the ongoing evolution of the business.

The Role of Innovation

1. Encourage Creative Thinking

Staying relevant often requires innovating beyond existing products or services. Encourage a creative mindset across your organization by facilitating brainstorming sessions and workshops focused on idea generation.

- **Cross-Pollination**: Promote collaboration between different departments to inspire innovative thinking. Diverse perspectives foster creativity and lead to unique solutions.

2. Invest in Research and Development

Allocate resources for research and development initiatives that focus on exploring new ideas or improving existing offerings. Invest in experiments that allow you to test new concepts and assess their viability.

- **Iterative Innovation**: Implement an iterative approach to innovation, where you continually refine and improve based on learnings. This not only enhances your offerings but also keeps your business agile and adaptable.

3. **Stay Connected to Your Industry**

Networking and engaging with industry peers can expose you to new ideas, best practices, and emerging trends. Join professional associations, attend conferences, and participate in industry discussions to stay connected and informed.

- **Collaborative Innovation**: Explore opportunities for collaboration with other businesses or entrepreneurs that can lead to innovative partnerships or projects. Working together can amplify your resources and knowledge.

As we conclude this chapter on staying relevant in a changing world, it is vital to acknowledge that adaptability is an essential trait for modern entrepreneurs. By committing to ongoing learning, engaging with customers, embracing technology, conducting thorough market analysis, and fostering a culture of innovation, you position yourself to weather the storms of change and thrive amid uncertainty.

Remember, the entrepreneurial journey is not static—it is a continuous evolution. Your ability to adapt and respond to emerging trends and shifts will determine your long-term success and impact. Embrace change as an opportunity for growth and innovation, rather than a threat to your stability. With the right strategies and mindset, you can transform potential challenges into avenues for advancement.

As you navigate the future of your entrepreneurial journey, keep your eyes open to the possibilities that arise from change. Staying relevant in a rapidly evolving landscape involves not just reacting to current trends but also anticipating future developments and positioning your business accordingly.

Reflection

Take a moment to evaluate your current approach to staying relevant in your industry. Are there areas where you can improve your adaptability and responsiveness to change? Consider the following questions:

- What recent changes have you observed in your industry, and how have they affected your business?

- How well are you engaging with your customers to gather insights about their needs and preferences?

- What steps can you take to enhance your understanding of emerging technologies that may impact your sector?

Write down three specific actions you will take in the coming weeks to enhance your adaptability and ensure that you remain relevant in the face of ongoing changes. Whether it's investing time in learning about new technologies, seeking customer feedback, or building a flexible culture within your organization, commit to a proactive approach that prepares you for the challenges and opportunities that lie ahead.

Chapter 30

The Joy of the Journey

Encouragement to enjoy the entrepreneurial process
and embrace each moment.

Entrepreneurship is often portrayed as a relentless pursuit of success, filled with hustle and hard work. This perception can overshadow an essential aspect of the entrepreneurial experience: the joy of the journey itself. While achieving goals and reaching milestones is undoubtedly fulfilling, it is the moments along the way—the challenges, the triumphs, the connections, and the lessons learned—that truly define the entrepreneurial adventure. In this chapter, we will explore the importance of embracing each moment in your journey, finding joy in the process, and cultivating a mindset that appreciates the richness of the entrepreneurial experience.

The Importance of the Journey

1. **Process Over Outcome**: It's easy to become fixated on end goals, losing sight of the process that leads to those achievements. Every step you take, whether forward or backward, contributes to your growth as an entrepreneur. Celebrate the little victories along the way, as they are the building blocks of your success.

2. **Learning from Experiences**: Every entrepreneur faces challenges—obstacles that test resilience, creativity, and adaptability. Rather than viewing these challenges solely as setbacks, embrace them as vital learning experiences. Each lesson learned

adds depth to your journey and equips you with insights that benefit your future endeavors.

3. **Cultivating Relationships**: The entrepreneurial journey is as much about the relationships you build as it is about the businesses you create. Engage meaningfully with peers, mentors, customers, and your team. These connections enrich your experience, providing support, collaboration, and inspiration that enhance the joy of the journey.

Strategies for Embracing the Joy of the Journey

1. Practice Mindfulness

Mindfulness—the practice of being present and fully engaged in the moment—can significantly enhance your experience as an entrepreneur. By cultivating mindfulness, you can appreciate the nuances of each step along the entrepreneurial path.

- **Daily Reflection**: Set aside time each day for reflection, where you can pause to acknowledge your experiences, feelings, and thoughts. This practice can help you savor not only successes but also the lessons learned through challenges.

- **Mindful Breaks**: Incorporate short mindful breaks into your workday. Whether it's a few minutes of deep breathing, a walk outside, or a moment of quiet contemplation, these breaks can help you recharge and re-center, allowing you to approach your work with renewed focus.

2. Celebrate Milestones and Achievements

Regularly celebrate both big and small milestones in your entrepreneurial journey. Acknowledging achievements reinforces your progress and encourages a positive mindset.

- **Create Rituals**: Establish rituals for celebrating achievements, such as team gatherings, personal reflections, or writing down successes in a journal. Celebrating milestones not only motivates you but also reinforces a culture of appreciation within your team.

3. Connect with Your "Why"

Constantly revisit and connect with the overarching purpose that drives your entrepreneurial journey. Understanding your "why" provides a deep sense of fulfillment and helps to reframe challenges in a more meaningful context.

- **Visual Reminders**: Use visual reminders of your mission and purpose, like posters or vision boards, to keep your motivation alive. When times get tough, referring back to your core values and goals can reignite your passion.

4. **Engage in Community and Giving Back**

Finding joy in the entrepreneurial process extends beyond individual success. Engage with your community, contribute positively, and give back.

- **Volunteer Opportunities**: Participate in community service or mentorship programs that allow you to share your expertise and make a difference. Giving back not only connects you with others but also enriches your sense of purpose and fulfillment.

5. **Practice Gratitude**

Incorporating gratitude into your daily routine enhances your overall experience and helps you appreciate the journey. Recognizing the positive aspects of your entrepreneurial path fosters a sense of joy and contentment.

- **Gratitude Journaling**: Maintain a gratitude journal where you record things you are thankful for each day—whether it's supportive colleagues, meaningful conversations, or enlightening experiences. This practice keeps your focus on the positive aspects of your journey.

The Lasting Impact of Joy in Your Journey

1. **Enhanced Resilience**: Embracing the joy of the journey helps build resilience. When you cultivate a positive perspective, you are better equipped to

handle setbacks, learning from them and bouncing back stronger.

2. **Stronger Team Culture**: Sharing joy and positivity within your team fosters camaraderie, collaboration, and motivation. When everyone embraces the journey together, it creates a thriving work culture that amplifies creativity and productivity.

3. **Sustained Passion**: A focus on the joy of the journey sustains your passion for entrepreneurship. The joy becomes intrinsic to your work, motivating you to continue pursuing your goals and nurturing a fulfilling entrepreneurial experience.

As we conclude this chapter on the joy of the journey, remember that entrepreneurship is not just about destinations and outcomes but about the experiences, relationships, and personal growth you encounter along the way. Every moment—whether filled with triumphs or trials—contributes to the tapestry of your entrepreneurial adventure. By embracing the journey, you cultivate a fulfilling experience that goes beyond financial success, enriching both your personal and professional life.

Prioritize finding joy in the small victories, the lessons learned, and the connections made. Celebrate your progress and acknowledge the hard work that has brought you to where you are today. Focus on the passion that inspired you to embark on this journey in the first place and remember that the true rewards of entrepreneurship lie not just in achieving milestones but in the joy found along the path.

Reflection

Take a moment to reflect on your entrepreneurial journey. Consider the following questions:

- What aspects of your journey have brought you the most joy and fulfillment?

- How can you better appreciate the moments—both good and challenging—that have shaped your experience?

- What steps can you take to ensure that you cultivate joy moving forward, even during tough times?

Write down your reflections and identify three specific actions you will commit to in order to embrace the joy of your entrepreneurial journey. Whether it's celebrating achievements, practicing gratitude, or creating moments of connection with your team, enjoy the process of building your dreams.

Manufactured by Amazon.ca
Bolton, ON

45119762R00116